RAFT 2035

Roadmap to Abundance, Flourishing, and Transcendence, by 2035

David W. Wood
Chair, London Futurists

Paperback ISBN 978-0-9954942-4-4

Published by Delta Wisdom

"It's often said that technology is poised to make humans stronger and more intelligent. But *RAFT* emphasises the possibility of a change that is much more important – the potential for technology to make us kinder and more empathetic. It's a message that deserves to be widely heard."

David Pearce, Philosopher,
and advocate of Paradise Engineering

"In *RAFT*, David Wood challenges all of us to reconsider how technology can best serve ethics, safety, and values that uplift the human spirit. A future that champions the very best aspects of what it means to be human is within our grasp, if we can humanise technology, and harmonize the interests of advanced civilization with nature."

Nell Watson, Chair of EthicsNet.org and IEEE's
Certification for Ethics in Transparency

"The need for a different set of politics is more pressing than ever. *RAFT* is a framework for the transition we need to make which is beyond the faultlines of traditional political positions."

Hannes Sjöblad, Co-founder DSruptive Sweden,
and Chief Disruptive Officer of Epicenter Stockholm

"By 2035, thanks to profound innovations in technology and society, human flourishing could be at a much higher level than at present. *RAFT* challenges all of us to seize the opportunity and to cooperate in building that future."

David Orban, Founder and Managing Partner,
Network Society Ventures

"This book offers clear messages on what is facing us and the importance of maintaining a holistic view of the future that includes everybody. Strong ethical points and social issues are addressed. The authors insight regarding 'what next?' is portrayed in realistic terms."

Karl Friðriksson and **Sævar Kristinsson**,
The Icelandic Center of Future Studies

"Anyone can say that the next decade will be crucial for humankind. But not everyone can provide smart and weighted solutions to the key problems humanity is facing. *RAFT 2035* does exactly that. It's a must read."

Kate Levchuk, Founder, Transpire

"*RAFT* is what the world needs! It empowers individuals to control their own destiny so they are not passive victims of the future, but can instead directly participate in creating a future world of abundance and human flourishing that benefits everyone."

Kim Solez, M.D., Director of Technology and the Future of Medicine Course at the University of Alberta, and Co-Chair Transplant Regenerative Medicine Community of Practice, American Society of Transplantation

"I've often enjoyed listening to David Wood set out his hopes and fears for the future. In *RAFT 2035* he applies his formidable insight to the very important question of securing a truly great future, for the United Kingdom and beyond, by 2035."

Matt O'Neill, Futurist Keynote Speaker, Futurist.Matt

"*RAFT 2035* maps out the possibilities and the trade-offs our exponential world is going to need. Continuing as before with tiny incremental steps is no longer an option: we need a RAFT of big ideas to make a step-change. Let's pick up these ideas and get on board for a brave new 2035."

Paul Imre, VP of Education, Data Science Speakers Club, Toastmasters International

Table of Contents

Welcome to the raft

Before the welcome, a word of warning. Buckle up. Prepare for wave after wave of turbulence.

The fifteen years from 2020 to 2035 could be the most turbulent of human history. Revolutions are gathering pace in four overlapping fields of technology: nanotech, biotech, infotech, and cognotech, or NBIC for short. In combination, these NBIC revolutions offer enormous new possibilities. These possibilities include enormous opportunities *alongside enormous risks*:

- **Nanotech** can provide resilient new materials, new processes for manufacturing and recycling, new ways to capture and distribute energy, new types of computing hardware, and pervasive new surveillance networks of all-seeing sensors.
- **Infotech** can augment human intelligence and creativity with new generations of artificial intelligence, leaping over human capabilities in increasing numbers of domains of thought, and displacing greater numbers of human employees from tasks which used to occupy large parts of their paid employment.
- **Biotech** enables the modification not only of nature, but of *human* nature: it will allow us not only to create new types of lifeform – synthetic organisms that can outperform those found in nature – but also to edit the human metabolism more radically than is possible via existing tools

such as vaccinations, antibiotics, and occasional organ transplants.

- **Cognotech** allows similar modifications for the human mind, brain, and spirit, enabling in just a few short weeks the kind of changes in mindset and inner character which previously might have required many years of disciplined study of yoga, meditation, and/or therapy; it also enables alarming new types of mind control and ego manipulation.

Rapid technological change tends to provoke a turbulent social reaction. Old certainties fade. New winners arrive on the scene, flaunting their power, and upturning previous networks of relationships. Within the general public, a sense of alienation and disruption mingles with a sense of profound possibility. Fear and hope jostle each other. Whilst some social metrics indicate major progress, others indicate major setbacks. The claim "You've never had it so good" coexists with the counterclaim "It's going to be worse than ever". To add to the bewilderment, there seems to be lots of evidence confirming *both* views.

The greater the pace of change, the more intense the dislocation. Due to the increased scale, speed, and global nature of the ongoing NBIC revolutions, the disruptions that followed in the wake of previous industrial revolutions – traumatic though they were – are likely to be dwarfed in comparison to what lies ahead.

Taming the turbulence

The forthcoming floods of technological and social change could turn our world upside down, more quickly and more brutally than we expected. When turbulent waters are bearing down fast, having a sturdy raft at hand can be the difference between life and death.

Turbulent times require a space for shelter and reflection, clear navigational vision despite the mists of uncertainty, and a powerful engine for us to pursue our own direction, rather than just being carried along by forces outside our control. In other words, turbulent times require a powerful "raft" – a roadmap to a future in which the extraordinary powers latent in NBIC technologies are used to raise humanity to new levels of flourishing, rather than driving us over some dreadful precipice.

To spell out the "RAFT" acronym, the turbulent times ahead require:

- A **Roadmap** ('R') – not just a lofty aspiration, but specific steps and interim targets
- towards **Abundance** ('A') for all – beyond a world of scarcity and conflict
- enabling **Flourishing** ('F') as never before – with life containing not just possessions, but enriched experiences, creativity, and meaning
- via **Transcendence** ('T') – since we won't be able to make progress by staying as we are.

The pages ahead describe such a roadmap. *Welcome!*

The world to come

How good could life become by 2035, if people really apply themselves to the task?

Here's the answer from RAFT 2035:

- Thanks to the thoughtful application of breakthroughs in science and technology, the future can be *profoundly better* than the present
- 2035 could see an *abundance of all-round human flourishing*, with no-one left behind.

The word "abundance" here means that there will be enough for everyone to have an excellent quality of life. No one will lack access to healthcare, accommodation, nourishment, essential material goods, information, education, social engagement, free expression, or artistic endeavour.

RAFT 2035 envisions the possibility, by 2035, of an abundance of human flourishing in each of six sectors of human life:

- Individual health and wellbeing
- The wellbeing of social relationships
- The quality of international relationships
- Sustainable relationships with the environment
- Humanity's exploration of the wider cosmos beyond the earth
- The health of our political systems.

RAFT offers clear goals for what can be accomplished in each of these six sectors by 2035 – 15 goals in total, for society to keep firmly in mind between now and that date.

The 15 goals each involve taking wise advantage of the remarkable capabilities of 21st century science and technology: robotics, biotech, neurotech, nanotech, greentech, artificial intelligence, collaboration technology, and much more.

The goals also highlight how the development and adoption of science and technology can, *and must*, be guided by the very best of human thinking and values.

Indeed, at the same time as RAFT 2035 upholds this vision, it is also fully aware of *deep problems and challenges* in each of the six sectors described.

Progress will depend on a growing number of people in all areas of society:

- Recognising the true scale of the opportunity ahead
- Setting aside distractions
- Building effective coalitions
- Taking appropriate positive actions.

These actions make up RAFT 2035. *There's plenty of work to be done!*

A world of difference

Here's what's different about RAFT compared to most other political visions.

- Most other political visions assume that only modest changes in the human condition will take place over the next few decades. In contrast, RAFT takes seriously the potential for large changes in the human condition – and sees these changes not only as *desirable* but *essential.*
- Most other political visions are preoccupied by short term incremental issues. In contrast, RAFT highlights major disruptive opportunities and risks ahead.

- Finally, most other political visions seek for society to "go back" to elements of a previous era, which is thought to be simpler, or purer, or in some other way preferable to the apparent messiness of today's world. In contrast, RAFT offers a bold vision of creating a new, much better society – a society that builds on the existing strengths of human knowledge, skills, and relationships, whilst leaving behind those aspects of the human condition which unnecessarily limit human flourishing.

It's an ambitious vision. But as the following chapters explain, there are many solutions and tools at hand, ready to energise and empower a growing coalition of activists, engineers, social entrepreneurs, researchers, creatives, humanitarians, and more.

These solutions can help us all to transcend our present-day preoccupations, our unnecessary divisions, our individual agendas, and our inherited human limitations.

Going forwards, these solutions mean that, with wise choices, constraints which have long overshadowed human existence can soon be lifted:

- Instead of physical decay and growing age-related infirmity, an abundance of health and longevity awaits us.
- Instead of collective foolishness and blinkered failures of reasoning, an abundance of intelligence and wisdom is within our reach.
- Instead of morbid depression and emotional alienation – instead of envy and egotism – we can

achieve an abundance of mental and spiritual wellbeing.

- Instead of a society laden with deception, abuses of power, and divisive factionalism, we can embrace an abundance of democracy – a flourishing of transparency, access, mutual support, collective insight, and opportunity for all, *with no one left behind.*

Why change can accelerate

RAFT envisions a huge amount of change taking place between the present day and 2035. What are the grounds for imagining this kind of change will be possible?

To be clear, there is nothing inevitable about any of the changes foreseen by RAFT. It is even possible that the pace of change will *slow down*:

- Due to a growing disregard for the principles of science and rationality
- Due to society placing its priorities in other areas
- Due to insufficient appetite to address hard engineering problems
- Due to any of a variety of reversals or collapses in the wellbeing of civilisation.

On the other hand, it's also possible that the pace of technological change as experienced by global society in the *last* 15 years – pace that is already breathtaking – could *accelerate* significantly in the *next* 15 years:

- Due to breakthroughs in some fields (e.g. AI or nanotechnology) leading to knock-on breakthroughs in other fields

- Due to a greater number of people around the world dedicating themselves to working on the relevant technologies, products, and services
- Due to more people around the world reaching higher levels of education than ever before, being networked together with unprecedented productivity, and therefore being able to build more quickly on each other's insights and findings
- Due to new levels of application of design skills, including redesigning the user interfaces to complex products, and redesigning social systems to enable faster progress with beneficial technologies
- Due to a growing public understanding of the potential for enormous benefits to arise from the NBIC technologies, provided resources are applied more wisely
- Due to governments deciding to take massive positive action to increase investment in areas that are otherwise experiencing blockages – this action can be considered as akin to a nation moving onto a wartime footing.

Interim targets

Importantly, for each of the 15 goals for 2035, RAFT recommends two interim actions to be progressed *between the present day and 2025*.

These interim targets are designed to establish what can be seen as three levels of "RAFT":

1. *Raised awareness of future technologies* – and awareness of the sweeping new powers these technologies will place in human hands
2. *Raised appreciation of the fast transformations* that can take place in human society in the wake of these new technological possibilities
3. *Raised anticipation of a forthcoming transcendence* – a transcendence in which humanity can soar beyond the limits which have hitherto cruelly stunted human experience.

This greater awareness, appreciation, and anticipation will arise from:

- Early demonstrations of the capabilities of solutions based on emerging new technologies
- A growing understanding of the operating principles of a society of abundance, flourishing, and transcendence
- Good answers to the objections that are sometimes raised against the ideas that make up RAFT.

As these interim targets are met, it will accelerate a growing change in public mindset, *and a growing desire to take further action.*

Evolution ahead

The content of RAFT 2035 has evolved via discussions in the global transhumanist community, particularly involving friends and supporters of the UK's Transhumanist Party. The ideas that follow are much larger than can be restricted to any one organisation or political party.

Accordingly, this roadmap is being published with the hope and intention that other social communities, political parties, and diverse think tanks can freely copy from it, adopting the RAFT ideas and analysis into their own platforms, and improving them.

If you like at least some of what you read, please consider stepping onto this RAFT, and helping to strengthen it, enlarge it, internationalise it, enhance the clarity of its navigational vision, boost its engine power, and prepare to welcome yet more participants.

For some specific ways to assist RAFT, please see the suggestions in the "FAQ" chapter towards the end of this book.

The goals previewed

The 15 goals contained in RAFT are split into the six sectors of human life already mentioned. The versions of the goals that follow are expressed as goals for people in the UK to keep in mind between now and 2035. Having one particular legislature in mind makes it easier to define concrete goals. Other versions of the goals can be developed for other locations around the world.

The first sector is new levels of **individual flourishing**. The goals here address bodily health and mental health:

1. The average healthspan in the UK will be at least 90 years (up from 63 as at present).
2. At least 99% of people in the UK will experience their mental health as "good" or "excellent".

The second sector is new levels of **social flourishing**. There are four goals in this sector:

3. Automation will remove the need for anyone to earn money by working.
4. There will be no homelessness and no involuntary hunger.
5. World-class life-preparation education to postgraduate level will be freely available to everyone.
6. The crime rate will have been reduced by at least 90%.

The third sector is new levels of **international flourishing**. There are two goals in this sector:

7. Risks of international military conflict will have been reduced by at least 90%.
8. The UK will be part of a global "free travel" community of at least 25% of the earth's population.

The fourth sector is new levels of **environmental flourishing**. There are three goals in this sector:

9. The UK will be carbon-neutral, thanks to improved green energy management.
10. The UK will be zero waste, and will have no adverse impact on the environment.
11. Consumption of meat from slaughtered animals will be cut by at least 90%.

The fifth sector is new levels of **cosmic flourishing**. There are two goals in this sector:

12. The UK will be part of an organisation that maintains a continuous human presence on Mars.
13. Fusion – the energy source of the stars – will be generating at least 1% of the energy used in the UK.

The sixth sector is new levels of **political flourishing**. The final two goals belong in this sector:

14. Politicians will no longer act in ways that are self-serving, untrustworthy, or incompetent. We'll all feel proud of our politicians, and grateful for them.
15. Parliament will involve a close partnership with a "House of AI" (or similar) revising chamber. Society will be guided by the best of human insight in close, productive collaboration with the best of AI insight.

The chapters that follow will look at the rationale for each of the goals, methods by which these goals can be accomplished, and, in each case, interim targets to be met by 2025.

As well as covering the individual goals, the chapters that follow will also highlight the important connections between the different goals. Indeed, progress towards any one of the goals will be under threat, unless there is good progress towards the other goals too. Conversely, progress for any one goal will tend to increase the likelihood of progress for the other goals.

Interconnections

In RAFT 2035 – as in so much of what is most valuable in life – *the whole is greater than the sum of the parts.*

To preview the interconnections between the six sectors, note the following:

Politics matters:

- Each of the RAFT goals can be accelerated by political leaders allocating sizeable chunks of public funds in support of key projects that are otherwise short of budget.
- Political leaders can put in place suitable incentives and subsidies to motivate entrepreneurs and businesses to focus on activities that the free market, left to its own profit-seeking mechanisms, would deprioritise.
- Incentives, subsidies, taxes, regulations, and other matters of political policy, can easily become counterproductive rather than productive; they may end up favouring vested interest groups rather than uplifting society as a whole. For this reason, politics needs to operate in ways that are lean, agile, open, and fully informed.

Individuals matter:

- Change cannot happen without individuals recognising the need for action, speaking up boldly, resisting naysayers, and applying a great deal of personal commitment to overcome resistance.
- Change initiatives can become frustrated, if individuals find their energy levels sagging, their thinking becoming confused, and their motivation dwindling. Change activists need to look after their own wellbeing, as well as keeping the bigger picture in mind.

- Change initiatives can be derailed if individuals allow their judgement to be clouded by feelings of hostility, vengeance, or self-importance. Change activists need to look after their emotional states as well as their physical health.

Communities and societies matter:

- As individuals, we draw strength and support from the communities to which we belong. Healthy communities make it more likely that individuals can perform at their best.
- Ideally, society will provide accommodation, nutrition, education, security, and many other elements that will assist change activists in their projects.
- In particular, society will, ideally, provide mentors, coaches, reviewers, facilitators, recruiters, and other human assistance, to magnify the effectiveness of individual change activists.

International relations matter:

- The challenges faced in any one locality often have mirror images elsewhere on the planet. Good international connections can enable promising ideas from one part of the globe to be brought to the attention of change activists worldwide.
- International influences can, alas, be negative as well as positive. Positive progress being made in one locale can be rendered irrelevant when issues elsewhere in the world spill over national borders and plunge new regions into chaos.

- Attempts to "close borders" are unlikely to be effective in a world with huge flows of data, finances, and ideas over wired and wireless networks. The battle for the best narratives and the best systems must take place globally, rather than just in a local context.

The environment matters:

- For each RAFT goal, it is insufficient to identify *sources of abundance* (for example, abundant food, or abundant energy), without considering whether these sources might become depleted. Instead, it is essential to consider practices that are *sustainable* – practices that will enable present-day flourishing without reducing the prospects for future flourishing.
- For each RAFT goal, it is insufficient to consider *human* flourishing. Instead, the implications should be considered for the other sentient and sapient minds with whom we share this planet.
- Nurtured well, and treated with respect, the natural environment can provide many wonderful experiences that can energise us and restore our balance, preparing us all to operate with greater effect in transforming those human structures which stand in the way of all-round flourishing.

The cosmos matters:

- The resources on the earth, whilst extensive, pale in comparison to those that exist elsewhere in the solar system, and in deeper regions of space. Our plans for the future can be transformed once we understand more fully both the cosmic opportunities and the cosmic risks of the wider universe.

- Most human life exists in what can be called "the base state of existence", but it seems likely that new dimensions of consciousness will be opened, as we transcend the current limits of the human condition.
- The destiny of humankind lies, not just on the earth as we know it today, but in vast new creations in both inner and outer space. Rather than being preoccupied by trying to "get back" to the living conditions of earlier human eras, humanity can find more powerful inspiration from a clearer picture of the abundance, flourishing, and transcendence which awaits us, in the stars as well as on terra firma.

Moving forwards

Good bodily health is the foundation for all other activities. As the start of the journey to an abundance of human flourishing, the next chapter highlights the remarkable progress that can take place in people's physical health by the year 2035.

1. Physical wellbeing

Goal 1 of RAFT 2035 is that **the average healthspan in the UK will be at least 90 years (up from 63 as at present)**.

The rationale for this goal is that good bodily health is the starting point for all other activities. Declining health diminishes human opportunities and curtails human freedoms, as bodies and minds become enfeebled. Declining health can also impose huge social and healthcare costs. Sadly, the healthcare budgets in countries all around the world are already creaking under severe stress.

However, there will be significant benefits, both socially and economically, to delaying the onset of chronic diseases of aging and thereby extending healthspan. These benefits are known as the "longevity dividend". Happily, these benefits now lie within our grasp.

Boosting healthspan

Healthspan has been defined as the amount of time an individual can live independently, without being hospitalised or requiring regular support from healthcare assistants or family or friends. It can also be measured as the amount of time that someone would assess their own health as being "good" or "very good".

The latest figures from the UK's Office of National Statistics[1] for expected *lifespan* in the UK are 82.9 years for women and 79.3 for men. The same data source states that *"healthy life expectancy"* is 63.6 years for females and 63.1

years for males. In other words, these figures predict that someone will, on average, be fully healthy for only 77 to 80% of their lifespan.

Unfortunately, the figures for expected healthspan are actually declining. For example, the expected healthspan for women has decreased by three months over a six year period (from 2009-11 to 2015-17).

But things don't need to be this way. We can look forward to three overlapping waves of improvements in how people age:

1. Technology that helps people to "age in place" better, so that, despite aging, people can lead fuller lives. This includes better monitoring systems to give early warnings of impending ill-health, better mobility solutions to reduce the need for people to rely on assistance, and better networking systems so that, despite diminished mobility, the elderly remain connected to their family and friends and have a rich social life.
2. Technology that enables more people to live like the "superagers" who age more slowly than the average person. A superager might live like they're 75, despite being 95 or older.
3. Technology that enables people to be "forever young" (if they choose it): they could live like they're 35, despite being 125 or older.

Learning from superagers

Superagers are defined as people who reach the age of 95 without being impacted by cancer, diabetes, cardiovascular disease, or cognitive decline. It's notable that superagers are often siblings or cousins of each other.

As well as aging more slowly, superagers tend to require less healthcare, even in the twilight years of their lives. They typically experience what is known as "compressed morbidity". A superager can utilise less medical budget throughout their long lives, in total, than a shorter lived neighbour who spends many more years in declining health.

A number of researchers are avidly studying superagers, to understand how they differ from the rest of the population, in terms of lifestyle, but also in terms of genetics and other biological features. The goal of this research is to understand what treatments and medical interventions might be made available to the rest of the population, so that superaging becomes the norm, rather than (as at present) the exception.

As well as learning from human superagers, it is possible to learn from a number of animal species that manifest various kinds of superaging, and even, in some cases, negligible senescence. Senescence refers to the trait, observed in humans and in most other species, that as we become older, we become more likely to die[2]:

- After the age of 35, for each additional eight years that we live, we become roughly twice as likely to die in the next 12 months.
- Stated otherwise, for every extra twenty five years that we live, we become roughly ten times as likely to die in the next 12 months.

However, there are some animal species that appear to demonstrate negligible senescence. In other words, animals in these species do not age. Their biology supports mechanisms that undo the wear-and-tear damage that normally accumulates as the years pass. Applying variants of these mechanisms within humans is a key quest of the emerging field of rejuvenation biotechnology.

Undoing aging

The root cause of age-related ill health is a set of different types of damage that accumulates over time at the cellular and molecular levels inside the body. By systematically repairing or reversing this damage, a substantial reduction should be possible in the prevalence of chronic diseases such as heart disease, cancer, dementia, stroke, and diabetes.

This is no empty theory. It is important to draw attention to the remarkable progress being made in the fields of regenerative medicine and rejuvenation biotechnology, and to the prospects for even faster progress in the years ahead. Thanks to a forthcoming suite of new biomedical interventions, the restorative biological properties that we presently experience in our youth, which generally enable us to bounce back quickly from injury or illness, will no longer lose their power as decades pass. Instead, it will become possible in the not-so-distant future to extend these restorative self-healing powers indefinitely, by taking advantage of biochemical and nanotech innovations such as nanosurgery, 3D bioprinting, genomic engineering, and stem cell therapies, in combination with personalised medical treatments enabled by machine learning of huge sets of medical data.

These restorative processes will not only be extended in their duration, but they will also grow in their scope and effectiveness. Diseases which formerly threatened even the most robust physical constitution will be cured more quickly. The destructive power of new pathogens will meet their match in the constructive restorative power of highly intelligent, swiftly adapting, personalised suites of biomedical therapies. And due to continuous monitoring of all our vital statistics, and of threats in our environment, corrective interventions can be triggered at much earlier stages in any downward spiral of bodily dysfunction.

These interventions will be an extension of the important principles of preventive and proactive healthcare – addressing issues at an early stage, before they become more complicated and expensive to treat.

The result will be like the regular visits we make to the dental hygienist that reduce the risk of gum and tooth disease – except that the set of diseases prevented by the periodic low-level bodily cleansing and repair will be much wider.

Progressing rejuvenation therapies

Examples of rejuvenation interventions already under investigation include[3]:

- Senolytics, a new class of compounds that remove from the body old and dysfunctional senescent cells (commonly described as "zombie cells")
- Treatments to selectively boost the natural autophagy ("self-eating") repair mechanisms that operate inside cells throughout the body
- Modifications to the microbiome – the set of microscopic bacteria, fungi, protozoa, and viruses that live in the human gut, on the human skin, and elsewhere inside the human body

- Infusions of stem cells – including cells harvested from placentas
- The application of the enzyme telomerase to extend the telomeres at the ends of chromosomes, effectively "resetting the clock" of the cells involved
- CRISPR reprogramming of cellular systems at both the genetic and epigenetic levels
- The use of specific hormones, including HGH (human growth hormone) and DHEA, to regenerate the thymus, thereby countering the age-related decline of the immune system (also known as immunosenescence)
- Mitoprotectants, including various antioxidant biomolecules such as NR/NMN and MITOQ, which can help to protect the mitochondria "power plants" of our cells.

What's more, a very useful role can be played by automation, machine learning, and testing within increasingly accurate computer simulations of biological systems. This means that existing natural and pharmaceutical compounds can be screened and evaluated for activity that may target key molecular processes involved in the repair of cellular and molecular damage.

To proceed more quickly, these initiatives deserve a greater share of society's resources to be applied to them.

It is encouraging to see the emergence of new investment mechanisms such as the Juvenescence[4] portfolio of companies developing treatments to extend healthspan. The founder of Juvenescence, Jim Mellon, comments as follows[5]:

> We aim to have about 20 shots on this goal – longevity science – and if we get two or three of them right, there will be a very good return to shareholders.

However, progress will be even faster with coordinated public action, along the lines advocated by the "Party for Health Research" (Partei für Gesundheitsforschung) political party in Germany[6]:

> The Party for Health Research would like to invest an additional one percent of the government's budget in the development of effective medicine against the diseases of old age. Because everyone is affected directly or indirectly by age-related diseases, everyone would benefit from this. To pay for this, one percent would be subtracted from each of the other budgetary items.
>
> Half of this additional money would go towards the construction and operation of new research facilities and the other half would be invested in training more scientists in the relevant fields. For this, the respective university departments would be extended.
>
> However, the faster development of effective medicine against age-related diseases is not only a question of solidarity and ethics. [Society] would also enjoy large economic benefits. Today's medical costs are already huge and will continue to grow with the upcoming demographic change. A reduction of age-related diseases would lead to an enormous economic benefit. Furthermore, this medicine against the diseases of old age will become the biggest industry ever as everybody needs it…

Quantifying the longevity dividend

If health systems in countries like the UK continue on their current trajectory, they're likely to bankrupt the whole country before long. It is not sustainable to continue to spend ever more money on existing treatment methods. Instead, a switch in focus, as recommended in this RAFT goal, is vital:

- A switch *away from* treating diseases only after they have already progressed to a serious extent
- A switch *to* early intervention and (even better) prevention.

What makes this switch possible is the paradigm change of targeting and treating metabolic aging as the common aggravating cause of multiple chronic diseases.

In broad terms, a contrast is clear between the economic and social consequences of two models of aging:

People in an unhealthy elderly state:

- Consume significant healthcare resources
- Contribute less to industry and community
- Impose a care-giving burden on family and friends.

People in a healthy elderly state:

- Don't consume so much healthcare resources
- Contribute more to industry and community
- Support and enrich their family and friends.

One attempt to quantify the economic size of the longevity dividend was made in 2013 by professors Dana Goldman, David Cutler, and collaborators, in an article entitled *Substantial Health And Economic Returns From Delayed Aging May Warrant A New Focus For Medical Research*[7]. The increases in life expectancy considered in this analysis are modest – only 2.2 years in a "delayed aging" scenario. However, what is striking is the financial consequence of this delay in aging. Aggregating expected costs from public programmes such as Medicare, Medicaid, Disability Insurance, Supplementary Security Premium, and so on, and including estimates for the productivity benefits from increased quality of life, the authors estimate the economic value of the delayed aging scenario to be 7.1 trillion US dollars, over the period up to 2060.

These benefits arise from two factors:

- A reduced number of disabled elderly people – as many as five million fewer, in the USA, for each of the years 2030-2060
- An increased number of non-disabled elderly people – up to ten million more, in the USA, over the same time period – resulting in greater contributions (both production and consumption) to the economy.

Inevitably, there's a great deal of uncertainty in the numbers quoted. However, even if the headline figure of $7.1 trillion is wrong by an order of magnitude, the upside remains compelling. And what's particularly interesting is that these benefits arise from such a small increment in life expectancy: just 2.2 years. *Imagine how much larger the benefits could be from a more sizeable increment.*

Interim targets

To accelerate progress towards Goal 1, two interim targets for 2025 are proposed.

1. A clear demonstration of mid-age rejuvenation of animals with much smaller lifespans than humans – animals such as mice in the first instance, and then pet dogs. Since these animals have short life

spans, experiments will take less time to show results. These demonstrations will change the public mood concerning the development of similar treatments for humans.

2. Establish a society-wide understanding of the principles of the longevity dividend, and of the measures that can be taken to quickly reduce the costs of rejuvenation therapies so that everyone can benefit from them. This understanding will defuse the fears that are sometimes expressed, that longer healthspans will result in significant problems for society or for the environment. This understanding will show that, on the contrary, longer human healthspans can have very good effects for both society and the environment.

The first interim target will help convince more people that extending healthspan is *possible*; the second interim target will help convince more people that extending healthspan is *desirable*.

Moving forwards

One of the fears that is sometimes expressed, regarding people having longer healthspans, is that increased physical robustness might be accompanied by decreased mental capability. In other words, individuals and, in their turn, social structures, might become forgetful, entrenched, and resistant to change. Human experience would be diminished, even though lifespans were extended.

However, RAFT 2035 envisions not only physical rejuvenation but also mental and spiritual rejuvenation. That's the subject of the next chapter.

For more information

- The annual conference *Undoing Aging*[8]
- The online community *Lifespan.io*[9]
- The *SENS Research Foundation*[10]
- The German "Party for Health Research"[11]
- The Longevity International[12] social enterprise
- The 2019 book by David Sinclair, *Lifespan: Why we age – and why we don't have to*[13]
- The 2019 book by Sonia Contera, *Nano Comes to Life: How Nanotechnology Is Transforming Medicine and the Future of Biology*[14]
- The 2019 book by James Clement, *The Switch: Ignite Your Metabolism with Intermittent Fasting, Protein Cycling, and Keto*[15]
- The 2019 update by S. Jay Olshansky, *The Longevity Dividend: A Brief Update*[16]
- The 2018 book by Kris Verburg, *The Longevity Code: The New Science of Aging*[17]
- The 2017 book by Jim Mellon, *Juvenescence: Investing in the Age of Longevity*[18]
- The 2016 book by David Wood, *The Abolition of Aging: The forthcoming radical extension of healthy human longevity*[19]
- The 2015 book by Anca Ioviţă, *The Aging Gap Between Species*[20]
- The 2007 book by SENS founder Aubrey de Grey, *Ending Aging: The rejuvenation breakthroughs that could reverse human aging in our lifetime*[21]
- Definitions of healthspan[22]

2. Mental wellbeing

Goal 2 of RAFT 2035 is that **at least 99% of people in the UK will experience their mental health as "good" or "excellent"**.

The statistics of people with mental health problems are collected and analysed every seven years by the Adult Psychiatric Morbidity Survey. Key findings from the most recent survey, which covered 2014, include the following[23]:

- During the year in question, around one man in every eight, and around one woman in every five, experienced a mental health problem
- Young women have emerged as a high-risk group, with high rates of common mental disorders and self-harm.

Out of the population as a whole, the rates of people experiencing particular mental health issues include[24]:

- 20.6% experienced suicidal thoughts at some time in their life
- 6.7% actually made a suicide attempt
- 7.3% harmed themselves
- 5.9% experienced generalised anxiety disorder
- 4.4% experienced PTSD (post traumatic stress disorder)
- 3.3% experienced antisocial personality disorder
- 2.4% experienced phobias
- 2.0% experienced bipolar disorder
- 1.3% experienced OCD (obsessive compulsive disorder).

In summary, far too many people nowadays suffer from deep depression, crippling anxiety, biting loneliness, distressing mood swings, and suicidal tendencies.

Harms caused by poor mental health

It may be argued that there are positive aspects to some of these psychological states – in other words, that it is wrong to classify so many people as having mental health problems. For example, some degree of stress and inner mental turmoil can be productive, in leading to positive personal transformation. However, in far too many cases, what people experience is stress that destroys character rather than builds it up.

Indeed, for men in England and Wales between the ages of 20 and 49, suicide is now the leading cause of death[25]. The WHO has predicted[26] that depression will be the single largest cause of disease burden worldwide by 2030. This is just the start of how poor mental health reduces the quality of human experiences.

Even when people don't report themselves as being mentally ill, they often fall victim to herd mentality, wilful deception by others, and self-deception, as well as manipulation by commercial factors or other social pressures. We are too prone to what are known, in polite language, as "cognitive biases" – and in plain language, as collective stupidity. We are misled by fake news, by clever flattery, and by carefully targeted individualised communications that prey on hopes and fears of which we ourselves are only dimly aware. Despite having clever brains with access to huge amounts of information, we frequently use our intelligence unwisely, finding arguments that appear to justify us staying in our current mental ruts, and clinging to these arguments through thick and thin.

Poor mental health has consequences not only for individuals but for society as a whole. Ill-judged actions arising from disturbed mental processing worsen social strains. Indeed, mental ill-health often leads to behaviour that is fanatical, fundamentalist, criminal, or socially divisive, as well as self-harming.

With people having easier access to various sorts of "weapons of mass destruction", the consequences of poor mental health become ever more serious.

It doesn't have to be like this. Twenty first century understanding of the brain and mind suggests a number of steps that can be pursued.

Beyond normal mental wellbeing

Bringing many more people up to what might be called "normal mental wellbeing" is only the beginning of what could be achieved. As a comparison, that outcome would be similar to a programme of better physical health, that allowed more people to live to the age of 80 years. That would be a very laudable outcome, but it's far short of what's actually possible. As covered in the previous chapter, rejuvenation biotechnology has the potential to enable much greater physical health for all, well beyond the age of 80. This is sometimes summarised as living "better than well".

As for physical health, so also for mental health. New technology has the potential to enable many more people to regularly reach levels of consciousness that previously were only occasionally reached, by a very small subset of the human population. These levels of consciousness involve deeper levels of calmness, compassion, connectedness, creativity, and much more.

Steps towards increased mental wellbeing

Steps towards increased mental wellbeing include:

- Greater access to mindfulness training, such as methods promoted by the Search Inside Yourself Leadership Institute
- Guided hypnosis, guided lucid dreaming, and guided meditations
- An improved understanding of the impact on mental health of diet, exercise, sleep, and interactions with nature, such as gardens and "forest bathing" (Shinrin Yoku)
- Increased access to therapists who practice an evidence-based therapy technique such as Cognitive Behavioural Therapy; this can happen via face-to-face interactions, online sessions, and/or suitable applications
- Education on mental health issues, in order to alleviate stigma
- Education about harmful effects of social media, and how to counter these effects
- Education about the evolutionary background of our cognitive biases and "wilful irrationality", and about how to rise above these self-sabotaging traits
- Potentially, wise use of selected psychedelics, as is being investigated by the Centre for Psychedelics Research at Imperial College, and by the

Multidisciplinary Association for Psychedelic Studies (MAPS)

- Monitoring of mental state, via biofeedback and other measurement systems
- The use of so-called "smart helmets" to deliver tDCS (transcranial direct current stimulation), or other electromagnetic stimulation
- Personalised "intelligent assistants" which can coach people regarding actions likely to affect their mental health
- Other "transformational technology" solutions being investigated and developed by the community of companies and organisations that are connected by Transtech Labs (this community focuses on solutions designed to "reduce psychological suffering" and/or "accelerate progress towards psychological wellbeing").

Moreover, these science-based tools and techniques that work on the individual level will be supported by a greater awareness of how mental wellbeing is deeply impacted by two sets of context.

The first context is our social circumstances, including relentless bombardment by advertising, regular reminders of the apparent stark inequalities within society, fear of falling behind or missing out, and worries related to money, relationships, and work. Our emotions are being stirred raw by problems within society. Addressing this context involves improvements in social wellbeing. These are covered in later parts of RAFT (Goals 3 through 6).

Mental wellbeing and personal narratives

The second context for our mental wellbeing is our personal philosophies, including the mental stories we tell ourselves, consciously and unconsciously – stories that are often pernicious and unhelpful.

Related to this is:

- A decline in the influence of the grand religious stories that we *used to* tell ourselves with confidence, but which can no longer provide the same kind of conviction
- A corresponding decline in the social activities of many churches, and a decline (as detailed by Robert Putnam in his book *Bowling Alone*[27]) in civic institutions
- A feeling (as expressed by Douglas Murray in *The Strange Death of Europe*[28]) of "existential tiredness" and "that the future has run out".

Renowned US general James Mattis – who is sometimes described as "warrior monk" – was asked on taking up the role of US Secretary of Defence about what worried him most in his new role. He answered as follows[29]:

> The lack of a fundamental friendliness. It seems like an awful lot of people in America and around the world feel spiritually and personally alienated, whether it be from organized religion or from local community school districts or from their governments...
>
> Go back to Ben Franklin – his descriptions about how the Iroquois Nations lived and worked together. Compare that to America today. I think that, when you look at veterans coming out of the wars, they're more

> and more just slapped in the face by that isolation, and they're used to something better. They think it's PTSD – which it can be – but it's really about alienation.
>
> If you lose any sense of being part of something bigger, then why should you care about your fellow-man?

Accordingly, a key factor in overcoming adverse mental patterns will be the rediscovery of a "sense of being part of something bigger", that is, a better self-vision for people to keep in their minds.

Step forward the positive RAFT vision of harnessing technological innovations to build a society with an abundance of human flourishing. Via the grand narrative, excitement, and sense of purpose that this vision provides, all of us can be helped to transcend and overcome self-destructive mental tendencies.

As Alex Evans of the Collective Psychology Project writes in his book *The Myth Gap*,

> In this time of global crisis and transition – mass migration, inequality, resource scarcity, and climate change – it is stories, rather than facts and pie-charts, that will animate us and bring us together. It is by finding new [narratives], those that speak to us of renewal and restoration, that we will navigate our way to a better future.

Interim targets

To accelerate progress towards Goal 2, two interim targets for 2025 are proposed:

1. A demonstration of long-lasting effectiveness of some of the proposed new "transformational technology" solutions for improved mental wellbeing. These demonstrations will change the

public mood concerning the development and wider application of such treatments.

2. Update the legislation which unnecessarily constrains the wise use of some of the transformational technology solutions – especially legislation covering psychedelic drugs and other psychoactive substances.

Moving forwards

As mentioned above, mental health can be adversely impacted by problems at the societal level. It is time to turn, in the next chapter, to the possibilities for much improved social flourishing.

For more information

- The Transtech Labs support network[30]
- The Search Inside Yourself Leadership Institute[31]
- The Centre for Psychedelics Research at Imperial College[32]
- The Multidisciplinary Association for Psychedelic Studies (MAPS)[33]
- The Consciousness Hacking community[34]
- The Collective Psychology Project[35]
- The Happier Lives Institute[36]
- The 2013 book by Jonathan Haidt, *The Righteous Mind: Why Good People Are Divided by Politics and Religion*[37]
- The 2017 book by Alex Evans, *The Myth Gap*[38]
- The 2017 book by Steven Kottler, *Stealing Fire*[39]
- The 2017 book by Matthew Walker, *Why We Sleep: Unlocking the Power of Sleep and Dreams*[40]

- The 2018 book by Michael Pollan, *How to Change Your Mind: What the New Science of Psychedelics Teaches Us About Consciousness, Dying, Addiction, Depression, and Transcendence*[41]

3. Automation and work

Goal 3 of RAFT 2035 is that **automation will remove the need for anyone to earn money by working**.

Sooner or later, increasingly powerful automation systems, including robotics and AI, will be able to take over an ever-growing number of work tasks from humans. This should be seen, not as a *threat* to the livelihood of employees, but as an *opportunity* for all of us to spend more time on matters of most interest to us. None of us should find ourselves spending time in labour that is back-breaking or soul-destroying, or in what we perceive as "bullshit jobs".

The threat to employment from automation has long been foretold. Up till now, these predictions seem to have been premature. People who have lost jobs in one occupation, due to automation, have been able to retrain to acquire jobs in new occupations. However, the closer that AI comes to AGI – the closer that artificial intelligence comes to possessing *general* capabilities in reasoning – the greater the credibility of the predictions of widespread unemployment. The closer that AI comes to AGI, the bigger the likely ensuing social disruption. Anticipating and managing this disruption will require significant changes to our social contract – the system by which people in society look after each other.

Even though we cannot be sure of the timescales, we can make the following prediction. As AI improves, it's going to become increasingly hard for people who are displaced from one job by automation, to quickly acquire new skills that will allow them to carry out a different job that has no short-term threat of also being automated. Therefore, sooner or later, more and more people are going to find themselves unexpectedly out of work – or if not *un*employed, *under*employed. Without an adequate social safety net, their standard of living is set to fall. If we're not careful, more and more people will experience a large blow to their self-esteem and self-confidence. There will be more and more alienation, emotional distress, and anger.

An outdated mindset

The mindset that currently prevails in society can be called "the primacy of paid employment": unless someone undertakes paid employment, they are a substandard person, who should be reproached or scorned.

Of course, societies already make many exceptions to this concept. Basic pension payments are provided to all citizens, so long as they are old enough, without them needing to continue working. Basic educational funding is provided to all citizens, within certain age boundaries, even if they have not started paid work yet. Basic healthcare treatment is, this time with no age limits, provided free of charge to all citizens, whether or not they have paid employment. And when someone has lost their job, public funding is available, for a while at least, to help them as they look for a new job.

As another exception to the primacy of paid employment, family members frequently look after one another. Larger groups of mutual assistance "friendly societies" developed in many cultures around the world, in which resources were pooled, in order to assist members of the group who had special needs.

This spirit of mutual support should be applauded. Without a social safety net, a powerful spirit of apprehension can arise. The fear of becoming detached from the basic means of human flourishing can cause people to become narrow-minded, grasping, and self-centred. The fear of losing out generates resentment and bitterness. It drives people into a scarcity mentality, in which any gain by some members of society is seen as requiring others in society to suffer exploitation. Adverse effects follow, not only in personal wealth, but in personal health; not only in self-esteem, but in the quality of social relationships.

Dangerous sentiments

Whilst increasing numbers of people are finding themselves in precarious circumstances, the media bombards them with images of other people seemingly enjoying life as never before. For a highly visible subset of society, life appears to be full of marvellous material goods and mesmerising experiences. In contrast, for those impacted by technological underemployment, there's a growing sense of unfairness and alienation. They perceive that the best opportunities of life are passing them by. They perceive themselves to be victims of how society is changing.

These sentiments render the populace all the more prone to being swayed by misleading theories about the causes of their predicament – theories that attribute their misfortune to scapegoats such as immigrants, rootless internationalists, modernists, multiculturalists, far-off bureaucrats, and so on. It's time to take back control, they are told.

The sentiment is valid, but the courses of action recommended are frequently naive and dangerous. Fast-talking Svengali figures evoke various fantastical visions of local sovereignty, of national destiny, of returning to a simpler past, of cultural homogeneity, of military glory, of religious revival, and of confounding the opinions of uppity experts. In their hearts, the populace often discern the drawbacks of these courses of action. But due to feelings of desperation, they think that it's nevertheless worth shaking up the whole political system. Against their better judgement, they allow themselves to be swayed by emotive distortions and base generalisations, and they cast their votes for various demagogues and autocrats – people who claim they should be immune from the normal democratic processes of checks and balances. Alas, instead of gaining control, the populace will actually lose control.

Indeed, we should deeply beware any social transformation programmes that ignore the accelerating disruption caused by pervasive automation and machine intelligence. Such programmes are likely to cause more harm than good. Unless they directly address the challenges of tech-driven underemployment, political initiatives will waste time, distract attention, squander resources, damage social systems that should be part of the real solution, and store up an even greater sense of unfairness and alienation.

An updated social contract

From the RAFT viewpoint, the requirement for people to seek paid employment belongs only to a temporary phase in the evolution of human culture. From now on, the basis for societies to be judged as effective or defective, shouldn't be the proportion of people who have positions of well-paid employment. Instead, it should be the proportion of people who can flourish, every single day of their lives.

Accordingly, RAFT foresees a stage-by-stage transformation of the social safety net – so that *all* members of society have access to the goods and services that are fundamental to an agreed base level of human flourishing.

RAFT therefore proposes the following high-level strategic direction for the economy: *prioritise the reduction of prices for all goods and services that are fundamental to human flourishing.*

This kind of reduction is already taking place for a range of different products, but there are too many other examples where prices are rising (or dropping too slowly).

In other words, the goal of the economy should no longer be to increase the GDP – the gross domestic product, made up of higher prices and greater commercial activity. Instead, the goal should be to reduce the costs of everything that is required for a good life, including housing, food, education, security, and much more. This will be part of taking full advantage of the emerging tech-driven abundance.

Accordingly, the pages ahead describe several sweeping transformations regarding the GDP measurement which is at the heart of how economies are managed today.

Spreading abundance

The end target of the above RAFT strategy is that *all* goods and services fundamental to human flourishing should have *zero* price. Three policies carried out in parallel will advance towards this target:

1. The policy of reducing underlying prices, step by step, via rapid adoption of improved automation.
2. The policy of providing public subsidies to alleviate whatever prices remain in place for these goods and services.
3. The policy of starting with an agreed basic set of goods and services, described by a "cost of living well" index, and step-by-step extending this set over time.

For those goods and services which carry prices above zero, combinations of three sorts of public subsidies can be made available:

- An unconditional payment, sometimes called a UBI – an unconditional basic income – can be made available to all citizens of the country.
- The UBI can be augmented by conditional payments, dependent on recipients fulfilling requirements agreed by society, such as, perhaps, education or community service.
- There can be individual payments for people with special needs, such as particular healthcare requirements.

These subsidies can be paid out of a public dividend harvested from the abundant shared commons of society's accomplishments – accomplishments which are increasingly enabled by remarkable twenty first century technologies. This abundance also arises from wise use of public assets such as land, the legal system, the educational system, the wireless spectrum, and so on.

The organisations who benefit the most from these shared resources should contribute equitably to the public "abundance dividend".

Harvesting the abundance dividend

In practical terms, payments in support of the abundance dividend can come from the following sources:

- Stronger measures to counter tax evasion, addressing issues exposed by the Panama Papers as well as unnecessary inconsistencies of different national tax systems
- Increased license fees and other "rents" paid by organisations who specially benefit from public assets such as land, the legal system, the educational system, the wireless spectrum, and so on
- Increased taxes on activities with negative externalities, such as a carbon tax for activities leading to greenhouse gas emissions, and a Tobin tax on excess short-term financial transactions
- A higher marginal tax on extreme income and/or wealth
- Reductions in budgets such as healthcare, prisons, and defence, where the needs should reduce once people's mental wellbeing has increased
- Reductions in the budget for the administration of currently over-complex means-tested benefits.

Interim targets

To accelerate progress with Goal 3, two interim targets for 2025 are proposed:

1. Agreement on an initial series of "cost of living well" indices. The intent is that the measured value of each index should decrease over time, approaching zero. The intent is also that, over time, more focus will be given to later indices in the series – indices that include a greater range of goods and services formerly regarded as "luxury". The intent is that the values of these indices should approach zero in due course too.
2. Agreement on the basic elements of a revised social contract in which paid employment loses the prime position it has in present-day society. Today, paid employment is viewed as being uniquely desirable: unless someone undertakes paid employment, society tends to regard them as a substandard person. That attitude was useful to society in the past. But in the future, we need new attitudes.

Moving forwards

The next chapter looks at how the idea of "spreading abundance" applies in the particular cases of housing and food.

For more information

- Chapter 4, "Work and purpose"[42], of the 2017 book by David Wood, *Transcending Politics*[43]

- The 2014 book by Peter Barnes, *With Liberty and Dividends for All: How to Save Our Middle Class When Jobs Don't Pay Enough*[44]
- The 2015 book by Martin Ford, *Rise of the Robots: Technology and the Threat of a Jobless Future*[45]
- The 2016 book by Calum Chace, *The Economic Singularity: Artificial intelligence and the Death of Capitalism*[46]
- The 2018 book by David Graeber, *Bullshit Jobs: A Theory*[47]
- The 2018 book by Nicolas Colin, *Hedge: A Greater Safety Net for the Entrepreneurial Age*[48]
- The 2018 book by Andrew Yang, *The War on Normal People: The Truth About America's Disappearing Jobs and Why Universal Basic Income Is Our Future*[49]
- The 2019 book by John Danaher, *Automation and Utopia: Human Flourishing in a World without Work*[50]
- The report by the Millennium Project, *Work/Technology 2050: Scenarios and Actions*[51]

4. Homelessness and hunger

Goal 4 of RAFT 2035 is that **there will be no homelessness and no involuntary hunger**.

Goal 4 can be seen as a special case of Goal 3. No one will need to obtain paid work in order to enjoy a life of abundant flourishing. Therefore, present-day problems such as homelessness and involuntary hunger must become things of the past.

After all, secure shelter and reliable access to nutritious sustenance form the basis for many other positive experiences in life.

A stark assessment

The situation in the United Kingdom is described in a November 2018 report by Professor Philip Alston, United Nations Special Rapporteur on extreme poverty and human rights[52]. Here's how the report starts:

> The UK is the world's fifth largest economy, it contains many areas of immense wealth, its capital is a leading centre of global finance, its entrepreneurs are innovative and agile, and despite the current political turmoil, it has a system of government that rightly remains the envy of much of the world. It thus seems patently unjust and contrary to British values that so many people are living in poverty. This is obvious to anyone who opens their eyes to see the immense growth in foodbanks and the queues waiting outside them, the people sleeping rough in the streets, the growth of homelessness, the sense of deep despair that leads even the Government to appoint a Minister for suicide prevention and civil society to report in depth on unheard of levels of

loneliness and isolation. And local authorities, especially in England, which perform vital roles in providing a real social safety net have been gutted by a series of government policies. Libraries have closed in record numbers, community and youth centres have been shrunk and underfunded, public spaces and buildings including parks and recreation centres have been sold off. While the labour and housing markets provide the crucial backdrop, the focus of this report is on the contribution made by social security and related policies.

The results? 14 million people, a fifth of the population, live in poverty. Four million of these are more than 50% below the poverty line, and 1.5 million are destitute, unable to afford basic essentials. The widely respected Institute for Fiscal Studies predicts a 7% rise in child poverty between 2015 and 2022, and various sources predict child poverty rates of as high as 40%. For almost one in every two children to be poor in twenty-first century Britain is not just a disgrace, but a social calamity and an economic disaster, all rolled into one.

But the full picture of low-income well-being in the UK cannot be captured by statistics alone. Its manifestations are clear for all to see. The country's most respected charitable groups, its leading think tanks, its parliamentary committees, independent authorities like the National Audit Office, and many others, have all drawn attention to the dramatic decline in the fortunes of the least well off in this country. But through it all, one actor has stubbornly resisted seeing the situation for what it is. The Government has remained determinedly in a state of denial. Even while devolved authorities in Scotland and Northern Ireland are frantically trying to devise ways to 'mitigate', or in other words counteract, at least the worst features of the Government's benefits policy, Ministers insisted to me that all is well and running according to plan. Some tweaks to basic policy have reluctantly been made, but there has been a determined resistance to change in response to the many problems which so many people at all levels have brought to my attention.

Also in November 2018, homelessness in the UK was reported as reaching a record high[53], with 170,000 families and individuals experiencing destitution. This includes 38,000 under-25s and 4,200 over-65s. What's worse, homelessness has increased every year since 2012.

The UK's homeless rate of around 0.46% of the population compares poorly[54] with that of many other countries, including Germany (0.37%), France (0.21%), Finland (0.13%), Spain (0.09%), Italy (0.08%), Norway (0.07%), Portugal (0.03%), South Korea (0.022%), and Japan (0.0039%). This gives confidence to the view that homelessness in the UK can be significantly reduced.

Addressing causes of homelessness

Many cases of homelessness arise, not from a shortage of available accommodation, but from individuals suffering psychological issues. This element of homelessness will be addressed by the measures in Goal 2 to significantly reduce mental health problems.

But a number of additional solutions are available to help abolish homelessness. First and foremost, the construction industry should be assessed, not just on its profits, but on its provision of affordable good quality homes – as part of the emerging tech-enabled abundance for all.

Consider the techniques used by the company Broad Sustainable Building, when it erected a 57-storey building in Changsha, capital city of Hunan province in China, in just 19 working days[55]. That's a rate of three storeys per day. Key to that speed was the use of prefabricated units.

Other important innovations in construction techniques that should be supported and accelerated include 3D printing, robotic construction, inspection by aerial drones, and new materials with unprecedented strength and resilience.

Similar techniques can be used, not just to construct new buildings where none presently exist, but also to refurbish existing buildings – regenerating them from undesirable hangovers from previous eras into attractive contemporary accommodation.

With sufficient political desire, these techniques offer the promise that prices for property over the next 15 years might follow the same remarkable downwards trajectory witnessed in many other product areas: TVs, personal computers, smartphones, kitchen appliances, home robotics kits, genetic testing services, and many types of clothing.

Addressing involuntary hunger

Just as for the construction industry, a similar transformation needs to take place in the food industry. Examples of methods that can be utilised to reduce food prices and improve food quality include vertical farming, algae production, and synthetic biology, along with the avoidance of unnecessary food waste.

A major complication here is the amount of misinformation regarding which foods are truly healthy. For example, many companies imply that their sugary, addictive, high-carbohydrate food products are, somehow, good for us. Genuinely useful health advice is frequently drowned out by waves of marketing from well-funded corporations who have unhealthy products to sell.

There also appears to be sharp divisions even between different medical experts as to what kind of diet is actually good for us. Controversies rage over different kinds of fat, different kinds of cholesterol, different kinds of meat, different kinds of sweetener, different kinds of wine, and so on. Given these ambiguities, it's no surprise that inventive advertising material is able to suggest all kinds of health benefits from products that are actually more likely to harm us than to benefit us.

This is an example of the critical importance of highlighting real scientific methods and findings, rather than people falling for what can be called "fake science". RAFT 2035 accordingly champions a greater focus on respect for science and objective data.

Beyond confrontation

In principle, biochemical innovations (including GMOs – genetically modified organisms) can improve the quality of food, at the same time as reducing the costs of producing that food. However, there is a risk that debate over these biochemical innovations will lose sight of the goal of increasing human flourishing. Instead, the debate will become dominated by other motivations, namely, on the one hand an obsession with financial profits, and on the other hand a countervailing obsessive distrust of commercial corporations.

The first part of this risk is that powerful agrochemical corporations will develop and market products that boost their financial bottom line, without adequate consideration of negative externalities from these products. The logic of short-term boosts in revenues will lead these corporations to suppress or throw doubt on any studies that query the wisdom of these products.

These corporations are skilled at placing into official regulatory bodies people who are sympathetic to corporate viewpoints. There is often an overly cosy relationship between regulatory bodies and the corporations they are meant to regulate, with managers from one side looking forward to future well-paid employment on the other side of that revolving door. In this way, big-spending corporations often "capture" their regulators, distorting their independence via a mixture of overt and covert pressures. The same corporations often allocate large budgets to lobbying efforts.

Another complicating factor is that politicians are inclined to favour "light touch" regulations. These politicians, often swayed by eloquent lobbyists, look favourably at jumps in profitability for the companies involved, because these jumps contribute to overall metrics of the performance of the economy – and because, in the absence of a more balanced set of metrics, society gives undue attention to statistics of economic growth. Unfortunately, light touch regulation often means ineffective regulation.

An excess of force in one direction often leads to an excessive reaction in the other direction. Because the agrochemical industry is perceived by many critics as being a dangerous obstruction to free enquiry and open discussion, these critics in turn often become implacable foes of the entire industry. Accusations and counter-accusations fly in both directions. Minds narrow as battle positions are championed.

In this adversarial situation, the points of valid science raised by supporters of the agrochemical industry tend to be brushed aside by critics, without proper acknowledgement of their validity. Conversely, the valid safety issues raised by critics tend to be brushed aside by industry supporters, under the rationale that these critics appear to be motivated by bitterness and negativity.

Rather than a hostile discussion, we need an open-minded consideration. Rather than an antagonistic conflict between pro-industry enthusiasts and risk-averse critics, we need to be able to appreciate and integrate the valid observations of all participants in the debate. Rather than a shouting match, what we need is the ability to appreciate and integrate multiple perspectives and insights. And rather than regulators and politicians being out-of-depth in this fast-moving landscape of ideas and innovations, we need to connect everyone to collective intelligence. In this way, healthier food – and desirable high quality housing – will be increasingly available at lower and lower costs.

Interim targets

To accelerate progress with Goal 4, two interim targets for 2025 are proposed:

1. Agree a replacement for the GDP index as the guiding light for evaluating the success of the economy. Rather than focusing on increasing the

financial value of goods produced and consumed, we need an alternative which better measures the basis for all-round human flourishing. (One good starting point for this work is the UK National Wellbeing Index[56], produced by the Office of National Statistics.)

2. Establish a reliable, respected source of information about the true health benefits and risks of different types of diet and different kinds of accommodation. Existing highly contentious arguments about, for example, the role that can be played by GMOs, should have the raw emotion and panic removed from them, so we can all see more clearly what are the real risks and real opportunities.

Moving forwards

Alongside good accommodation and good nutrition, access to good education is another basic foundation for people to be able to flourish. The next chapter looks at how the ideas of "spreading abundance" can provide free world-class education to all.

For more information

- Chapter 6, "Towards abundant food"[57], of the 2019 book by David Wood, *Sustainable Superabundance*[58]
- Analysis by The Economist: *Home ownership is the West's biggest economic-policy mistake*[59]
- The BuiltInCommon community that "uses new technology to facilitate local fabrication of homes"[60]

- The 2018 book by Charles Mann, *The Wizard and the Prophet: Two Remarkable Scientists and Their Dueling Visions to Shape Tomorrow's World*[61]
- The 2017 book by McKay Jenkins, *Food Fight: GMOs and the Future of the American Diet*[62]
- The 2013 book by Eric Drexler, *Radical Abundance: How a Revolution in Nanotechnology Will Change Civilization*[63]
- The 2012 book by Peter Diamandis and Steven Kotler, *Abundance: The Future Is Better Than You Think*[64]

5. Elevating education

Goal 5 of RAFT 2035 is that **world-class life-preparation education to postgraduate level will be freely available to everyone**.

Goal 5, like Goal 4, can be seen as a special case of Goal 3. No one will need to obtain paid work in order to enjoy a life of abundant flourishing. Therefore, world-class life-preparation education should be available as widely and freely as possible.

Done well, education opens many new vistas, by providing valuable information, skills, and connections. It reduces the chances of people being misled or manipulated, or falling victim to deception or distortion. It prepares people better for activities that are more challenging but also more fulfilling. This kind of education badly needs to become available more widely and more fully.

Accelerating edtech

Just as for good accommodation and good food, what will make good education widely available will be to embrace the full potential of automation, including AI.

The associated technologies are sometimes called "edtech". This includes:

- An expansion of online materials and online courses
- Tech-supported collaborative learning
- AI systems, including automated essay marking, which can improve the evaluation of the areas in

which each student would benefit from further study and/or alternative approaches

- "Precision personalised education" – akin to "precision personalised medicine"
- Use of biofeedback to monitor and manage mental states while learning
- Opportunities with gamification and "serious games"
- Immersive virtual reality learning environments
- Time-shifted education, to counteract the "social jet lag" experienced by teenagers
- Empirical measurements of the effectiveness of different approaches to education.

Thanks to this kind of forthcoming improvements in edtech, there is no reason for education to be anything like as expensive as at present.

Edtech can transform, not only how educational materials are delivered and received, but also the content and structure of those educational materials, and, therefore, the ease of updating that material. The greater agility enabled by edtech will allow older educational material to be replaced more quickly by newer material that is more relevant for the fast-changing challenges ahead.

In parallel with increased use of edtech, the main role of human teachers will change from knowledge conduit to mentor.

A syllabus fit for the future

Education has traditionally focused heavily on preparing students for the workforce. Other goals, such as helping to develop human character, and preparing students for adulthood in general, have tended in practice to play a secondary role.

Indeed, present-day education tends to prepare students for the challenges of the past, when the needs and expectations of society were relatively stable. However, as the 2020s unfold, society is experiencing a confluence of five accelerating transformations:

First, people typically change their occupational role more frequently than in the past – when many spent their entire careers within a single company, or if not a single company, then in a single profession. What's more, a larger part of most people's lives will be spent outside of paid employment. A larger proportion of education should, therefore, be preparing students to thrive, not in work, but in a post-work society.

Second, people are being bombarded with ever-greater amounts of information, in rapidly evolving formats – with much of that information being *designed* to mislead or confuse, and lots more being *unintentionally* misleading or confusing. Accordingly, a focus on critical thinking and collaborative intelligence is sorely needed. This is in contrast with previous educational models which prioritised the memorisation of facts.

Third, emerging disruptive technology has the potential to transform human experience in multiple ways that are hard to predict, including ways that are wonderfully positive, as well as ways that are deeply negative. In contrast to previous educational models which tended to assume that most change is linear (incremental), education needs to do more to raise awareness of exponential change and accelerating feedback cycles. In particular, it's critical that education covers the skills of radical foresight, scenario design, and the identification and management of both existential risks and existential opportunities (that is, risks and opportunities that would profoundly alter the circumstances of human existence).

Fourth, interactions with other people aren't just more *numerous* than in the past, but are also more *diverse* – because of greater global travel and interaction than in the past; and because groups of people are increasingly adopting new lifestyles, new bodily modifications, new social structures, and new philosophies. Indeed, as well as coexisting with diverse other people, there will be a growing set of issues around coexisting with advanced AIs and robots. In contrast to previous educational models which assumed a broadly static cultural background, education now needs to prepare students for ultra-diversity.

Fifth, many of the assumptions behind traditional frameworks for ethics and morality are being challenged by new ideas that are circulating, and by unprecedented new possibilities that technology puts in our hands. Again, that's a reason for improved fluidity and clarity of thinking. It's a reason for education to regard not only IQ (measures of raw intellectual power) but also EQ, including emotional resilience and mental agility.

Taken together, these five ongoing transformations demand a corresponding change in the education syllabus – the cultivation of education that elevates rather than constrains.

In summary, it is time to re-evaluate much of the content of existing educational courses. These courses should be targeted at assisting students to cope with the pace of change in society, to reach their full potential, to identify and respond to opportunities and risks, and to participate wisely in social activities, including democratic decision-making. Thanks to edtech, these courses should be freely available to everyone.

Education improving

Due to the conservative nature of much of the educational establishment, it is to be expected that disruptive uses of edtech will tend to be pioneered in groups and organisations outside of the educational mainstream. Some encouraging examples should be noted:

- The free online courses available from Khan Academy[65]
- Mobile applications such as DuoLingo[66] which are teaching languages to unprecedented numbers of students worldwide
- The Ecole 42[67] initiative and partner colleges around the world
- The School of Life[68] with its extensive resources to "help people lead more fulfilled lives".

Once more public resources are deployed to support this kind of initiative, these courses will reach larger audiences, and cover a wider range of skills.

Interim targets

To accelerate progress with Goal 5, two interim targets for 2025 are proposed:

1. Clearly demonstrate the effectiveness of at least some elements of edtech, in reducing costs whilst delivering higher quality education. These

demonstrations will change the public mood concerning the usefulness, the development, and the wider application of edtech.

2. Reach agreement on the core of a transformed educational syllabus focused on new life opportunities – an education fit for the 2020s and beyond – an education that will, as it happens, equip members of society to make more rapid progress with the RAFT goals.

Moving forwards

Our social environment contains threats as well as opportunities. A threat which can unexpectedly derail someone's life is that of criminal attack, including violent assault, the theft or destruction of key possessions, and damage to personal reputation. The next chapter considers how this threat can be significantly reduced.

For more information

- The 2018 book by Yuval Noah Harari, *21 Lessons for the 21st Century*[69]
- The EdTech Digest[70]
- The 2008 book by Clayton M. Christensen, Michael B. Horn, and Curtis W. Johnson, *Disrupting Class: How Disruptive Innovation Will Change the Way the World Learns*[71]
- The 6 minute video by rapper "Prince Ea", *I sued the school system*[72]
- The RSA Animate video featuring Ken Robinson, *Changing Education Paradigms*[73]

6. Reducing crime

Goal 6 of RAFT 2035 is that **the crime rate will have been reduced by at least 90%**.

Compared to the previous goals in this group, Goal 6 looks at a different reason why lives can be stunted or damaged. It's when people become victims of crime, including violent crime, financial crime, or reputational crime. All of these types of crime can diminish the possibilities open to the people who are victims.

Indeed, security is a vital component in the foundational levels of people's overall hierarchy of needs.

Reducing the rate of crime involves addressing the causes of crime as well as the mechanisms of crime.

The primary goal here is to reduce the social and psychological pressures which incline people to commit criminal acts. This reduction in inclination towards criminal acts can be achieved, not by making people more docile or passive, but by providing everyone with strong incentives to channel their energy in ways benefiting society as a whole.

Crime statistics

Statistics on crime in England and Wales are available in the CSEW (Crime Survey for England and Wales) from the ONS (Office of National Statistics). A report published in April 2019[74] reviewed data on crimes up to December 2018, and going back as far as 1981. Here is the executive summary:

> Over recent decades we have seen continued falls in overall levels of crime but in the last year there has been no significant change. However, it is important to look at individual crime types as the total figure hides variation both within and across crime types. We have seen a rise in overall theft but a mixed picture in different types of offences involving theft. There are also differences in the lower-volume but higher-harm types of violence, with increases in homicide and offences involving knives and sharp instruments but decreases in offences involving firearms.

The report also highlights some caveats:

> An increase in the number of crimes recorded by the police does not necessarily mean the level of crime has increased.
>
> For many types of crime, police recorded crime statistics do not provide a reliable measure of levels or trends in crime as they only cover crimes that come to the attention of the police.
>
> Police recorded crime can be affected by changes in policing activity and recording practice and by willingness of victims to report.
>
> The CSEW does not cover crimes against businesses or those not resident in households and is not well-suited to measuring trends in some of the more harmful crimes that occur in relatively low volumes.

Adding up all the offences recorded in the different categories of crime, the total crime level of 1981 is estimated at around 11 million offences. This grew to a peak of around 20 million offences in 1995 before falling back in more recent years to between 7 million and 10 million offences per year. However, data for "computer misuse" has been introduced since 2018 and pushes up the most recent totals to around 11 million.

Crimes evidently vary in terms of their seriousness, and it would be a mistake simply to focus on numbers of offences. Moreover, the goal of reducing crime rates should not be met simply by some kind of reclassification, in which incidents previously regarded as crimes are somehow disregarded.

Reducing the causes of crime

RAFT 2035 initiatives to improve mental health (Goal 2), to eliminate homelessness (Goal 4), and to remove the need to work to earn an income (Goal 3), should all contribute to reducing the social and psychological pressures that lead to criminal acts.

However, even if only a small proportion of the population remain inclined to criminal acts, the overall crime rate could still remain far too high. That's because small groups of people will be able to take advantage of technology to carry out lots of crime in parallel – via systems such as "ransomware as a service", or "intelligent malware as a service", or worse. The ability of technology to multiply human power means that just a few people with criminal intent could give rise to huge amounts of devastating crime.

This raises the priority for software systems and the rest of our social infrastructure to be highly secure and reliable, so that they cannot be hacked.

Towards trustable monitoring

This also raises the priority of intelligent trusted surveillance of the actions of people who might carry out crimes. This last measure is potentially controversial, since it allows part of society to monitor citizens in a way that could be considered deeply intrusive. For this reason, access to this surveillance data will need to be restricted to trustworthy parts of the overall public apparatus – similar to the way that doctors are uniquely trusted with sensitive medical information. In turn, this highlights the importance of initiatives that increase the trustworthiness of key elements of our national infrastructure.

It remains an open question whether this increase in trustworthiness is achieved using new technology such as federated learning and blockchain, by alterations in social structures, or by other means.

Interim targets

To accelerate progress with Goal 6, two targets for 2025 are proposed:

1. Agree basic principles of the design and operation of systems for "trustable monitoring".
2. Advance practical initiatives to understand and reduce particular types of crime, starting with the types of crime (such as violent crime) that have the biggest negative impact on people's lives. For example, it is possible that legalisation of selected psychedelic drugs could lower the likelihood of gang warfare over the distribution of the same drugs, in turn reducing the prevalence of knife crime in the UK.

Moving forwards

Alongside the risks of damage inflicted from people or groups with criminal intent, we also need to address the risks of damage inflicted by international military conflict. That's the subject of the next chapter.

For more information

- The 2018 book by Bruce Schneier, *Click Here to Kill Everybody: Security and Survival in a Hyper-connected World*[75]
- The 2015 book by Marc Goodman, *Future Crimes: Everything Is Connected, Everyone Is Vulnerable, and What We Can Do About It*[76]
- The 1998 book by David Brin, *The Transparent Society: Will Technology Force Us to Choose Between Privacy and Freedom?*[77]

7. International conflict

Goal 7 of RAFT 2035 is that **risks of international military conflict will have been reduced by at least 90%**.

Goal 7 can be seen as an international version of Goal 6. Both these goals address the risks to human flourishing from violence and other crime. Goal 6 is for a 90% reduction of crime at local and national levels. Goal 7 considers the threat of violence and warfare at the international level.

In a world with ever more people having access to ever more powerful weapons, escalating conflict could bring civilisation to an end. Alongside possible attacks from other countries, we also need to consider threats from terrorist groups, international crime syndicates, and other sub-state organisations.

Some of these groups may initiate actions for reasons we might judge to be deluded, misinformed, hasty, suicidal, or mad in some other way. However, these actions may still take place, despite the various sorts of insanity that would be involved. It would be like a repeat of the cascade of unintended consequences that led Europe in 1914 into the horrors of the first world war, following a period in which many people thought, wrongly as it turned out, that large-scale war had become a thing of the past.

However, the increased spread of nuclear technology, chemical weapons, biological pathogens, and cyberattack capabilities, means that a similar cascade of actions in our time could have consequences that are even more devastating than the carnage of the first world war.

This state of affairs is sometimes given the semi-whimsical name "Moore's Law of Mad Scientists", on a suggestion from researcher Eliezer Yudkowsky[78]:

> The minimum IQ required to destroy the world drops by one point every 18 months.

This is a threat that deserves very serious attention, to prevent international society from sleepwalking into disaster.

Building trust

One response to the threat of attack is to increase spending on defence budgets. Unfortunately, this would mean that significant portions of national resources are tied up in military forces, preventing their deployment on other uses that would be more productive. Moreover, when a potential attacker perceives that it is facing stronger defences, it can prompt further spending on increased aggressive capability, ratcheting an arms race. Any short-term perceived gains in security would likely be illusory.

It would be far better to deescalate current and future threat situations, through measures to build and sustain mutual trust. That is what RAFT envisions.

One factor that can reduce pressures towards conflict is an increased general understanding of the scale of abundance that lies ahead, as humanity takes fuller advantage of green technologies, nanotechnology, robotics, artificial intelligence, and other technological breakthroughs. These technologies have the potential to allow every person on earth to have a significantly higher standard of living than was available even to royalty only a few decades ago. This understanding should reduce the pressures on different groups to compete against each other for a larger slice of the pie. The pie will be large enough for everyone.

However, the mere fact of material abundance is insufficient, by itself, to prevent conflict and strife. There are other causes of conflict, including differences in ideology, inertia from runaway arms races, the perception of inflammatory insults, and other aspects of emotional immaturity. These are all factors that need to be handled better. Happily, these are all factors that *can* be handled better, via RAFT initiatives.

Rejuvenating international liaisons

In principle, multilateral institutions can help to counter divisive forces, but today's United Nations and related organisations are falling far short of their potential in this regard. These organisations are overdue rejuvenation, starting with an update for the documents that define their purpose and operation. This refresh will clarify the potential beneficial role of the United Nations and related organisations in the world of the 2020s and beyond.

Regular exchanges between members of different groups from around the world, if skilfully facilitated, can also play an important role in deepening rapport and building trust. In the past, these exchanges involved international travel, but technologies such as immersive video conferencing can produce similar results at much lower costs. These online gatherings can and should be extended, to help more people escape from the mental shackles of constricting ideologies and backward-looking group-think.

International trustable monitoring

As in the case of Goal 6 – the reduction of crime by at least 90% – success with Goal 7 will require improved systems of trustable monitoring. This monitoring can take advantage of improved AI to identify latent aggressive intent or potential pathways of unintended conflict escalation. Again as for Goal 6, these systems will need to become "above suspicion", being respected by all parties. If their design and operation is transparent, such an outcome is more likely.

One particular challenge that international trustable monitoring needs to address is the risk of more ever powerful weapons systems being placed under autonomous control by AI systems. New weapons systems, such as swarms of miniature drones, increasingly change their configuration at speeds faster than human reactions can follow. This will lead to increased pressures to transfer control of these systems, at critical moments, from human overseers to AI algorithms. Each individual step along the journey from total human oversight to minimal human oversight might be justified, on grounds of a balance of risk and reward. However, that series of individual decisions adds up to an overall change that is highly dangerous, given the potential for unforeseen defects or design flaws in the AI algorithms being used.

Note that there can be agreement on at least some elements of trustable monitoring between groups that harbour considerable suspicion and antagonism towards each other. Consider how all commercial airliners contain a black box recording device. Rather than regarding this device as "snooping", members of the airline industry understand the benefits to everyone from good records being made, which can be consulted in the event of airplane accidents, in order to improve aircraft safety. International agreements on air traffic control meet the same general pattern: all countries benefit from these agreements. Likewise the organisation of international post, international sports competitions, and lots more besides. The challenge will be to apply relevant positive principles from these fields in the more unstable field of international military conflict.

Interim targets

To accelerate progress with Goal 7, two targets for 2025 are proposed:

1. Agree basic principles of the design and operation of systems for "international trustable monitoring". Among other points, this should highlight measures to constrain any runaway escalation of adoption of lethal autonomous weapons.
2. Establish a commitment from a majority of the countries in the United Nations to an updated version of the Universal Declaration of Human Rights which takes fully into account the remarkable transformational nature of the technologies highlighted in RAFT. It may take some time, subsequently, for this commitment to be backed up by action, but an agreement on basic principles will at least provide a start.

Moving forwards

As mentioned, one way to build trust across international borders is to increase the flow of personnel across these borders – in a managed way which avoids destabilising any of the countries involved. What this could mean in practice is the subject of the next chapter.

For more information

- The 2019 book by Paul Scharre, *Army of None: Autonomous Weapons and the Future of War*[79]
- A 2018 discussion between Paul Scharre, Stuart Russell, Anthony Aguirre, Ariel Conn, and Max Tegmark, *Why You Should Fear "Slaughterbots"*[80]
- The 2013 book by Ian Goldin, *Divided Nations: Why Global Governance Is Failing, and What We Can Do about It*[81]

8. Open borders

Goal 8 of RAFT 2035 is that **the UK will be part of a global "free travel" community of at least 25% of the earth's population**.

Freedom of movement means that people can travel to other locations in order to study, to work, to explore, to carry out joint projects, to deepen mutual understanding, or to engage in many other types of activity.

Greater freedom of movement can bring many benefits, including the building of the all-important trust and rapport mentioned in Goal 7. Migration has been found to have considerable net positive effects for the UK, including raising productivity, boosting public finances, strengthening cultural richness, and increasing individuals' well-being. Flows of money and ideas in the reverse direction also benefit the original countries of the immigrants.

Indeed, greater freedom of movement can assist with fulfilment at multiple levels of the hierarchy of human needs, including belonging and love needs, cognitive needs, aesthetic needs, self-actualisation, and transcendence.

Benefits quantified

Eight years of research by the Migration Advisory Council[82] (MAC) is summarised in a recent report by Professor Jonathan Portes of King's College London. Here are some extracts[83]:

> Immigration has a substantial, positive and significant on productivity; an increase in the immigrant share of the labour force by 1 percentage point is associated with an increase in overall productivity of 2 to 3 percentage points.
>
> Overall immigrants are relatively more beneficial for the public finances than natives, with migrants from the EU making on average a large positive contribution… On average, the average net fiscal contribution of an immigrant was £440 more than that of a native.
>
> The average EEA migrant arriving in 2016 will contribute a discounted total of around £78,000 to the UK public finances over his or her lifetime. Overall, the future net contribution of 2016 arrivals alone to the UK public finances is estimated at £25bn. Had there been no immigration at all in 2016, the rest of us would have had, over time, to find £25bn, through higher taxes, public service cuts, or higher borrowing.

The report notes that similar conclusions have been reached by international bodies such as the IMF and the OECD.

The case for open borders is also reviewed in an Economist article from July 2017 with the headline "A world of free movement would be $78 trillion richer"[84]. Here are some of the points from that article:

> In America, the foreign-born are only a fifth as likely to be incarcerated as the native-born…
>
> A study of migration flows among 145 countries between 1970 and 2000 by researchers at the University of Warwick found that migration was more likely to reduce terrorism than increase it, largely because migration fosters economic growth.

Borders, open but managed

However, unrestricted freedom of movement can lead to overcrowding, overuse or spoiling of local resources, the unwelcome disruption of previous cultures, and a rise in resentment and hostility between original residents and newcomers. That's why freedom of movement often faces opposition. For these reasons, systems of "free travel" and "open borders" necessarily involve a number of agreements and restrictions.

This is an example of an important general principle: in order to obtain and enjoy greater freedoms, various elements of lesser freedoms sometimes need to be restricted. For example, to enjoy the freedom to drive a car on a public roadway, we have to give up our freedom to drive at excess speed, or in a vehicle that has failed tests of roadworthiness, or whilst we are intoxicated. Likewise, to enjoy the freedom to travel to a different country, we have to give up our freedom to violate local laws or trample key local customs.

Similarly, to enjoy the full benefits of a rich association with a larger group of countries, the UK needs to be willing to adopt and support some standards agreed by the group as a whole. We need to be willing to pool sovereignty and to collaborate on decision-making, in order to gain more from the relationship than we lose.

Here are some examples of rules that could apply for international travel, to avoid any drastic adverse changes in local culture or social stability:

- Visitors could lose their right of residency if they fail to respect agreed norms.

- Immigrants could be denied a vote until they had been resident for a given amount of time (perhaps five years).
- Immigrants could be denied access to various social security payments (including any basic income payment) until, again, an agreed period of time has elapsed.
- Immigration of this sort could be restricted to people coming from countries with whom a reciprocal agreement exists.
- Immigration to particular regions of countries could be limited to numbers agreed in advance.

The growth of open border agreements

Recognising both the potential benefits and the potential drawbacks of free movement across open borders, a number of international open border agreements have been established around the world in recent decades, involving in each case a set of neighbouring countries which have a broad level of social alignment and economic equality with each other. Over time, as a sign of the general success of the idea, some of these regions have grown and merged[85].

Here are some examples from Europe:

- The Nordic Passport Union of 1954, establishing open borders between Denmark, Norway, Sweden, Finland, and Iceland.
- The Benelux Economic Union, dating from 1944, between Belgium, the Netherlands, and Luxembourg.

- The Schengen Agreement started in 1985 when the three countries of the Benelux Economic Union were joined by France and Germany in a declared intent to gradually remove checks for people and vehicles crossing the borders between these countries.
- The Schengen Agreement was subsequently extended to incorporate the countries of the Nordic Passport Union and also Austria, Czechia, Estonia, Greece, Hungary, Italy, Latvia, Liechtenstein, Lithuania, Malta, Monaco, Poland, Portugal, San Marino, Slovakia, Slovenia, Spain, Switzerland, and Vatican City.

Other examples from around the world can also be mentioned.

- The Andean Community in South America, dating from 2007, of Bolivia, Colombia, Ecuador, and Peru.
- The CA4 Border Control Agreement in Central America, dating from 2006, of El Salvador, Guatemala, Honduras, and Nicaragua.
- The CARICOM Single Market and Economy, in the West Indies, dating from 2009, of Antigua and Barbuda, Bahamas, Barbados, Belize, Dominica, Grenada, Guyana, Haiti, Jamaica, Montserrat, St Kitts and Nevis, Saint Lucia, St Vincent and the Grenadines, Suriname, and Trinidad and Tobago.
- The East African Community, dating from 2000, of Burundi, Kenya, Rwanda, South Sudan, Tanzania, and Uganda.

- The Gulf Cooperation Council, dating from 1981, of Bahrain, Kuwait, Oman, Qatar, Saudi-Arabia, and United Arab Emirates.
- The Trans-Tasman Travel Arrangement, dating from 1973, of Australia and New Zealand.
- And, at the time of writing, a common travel area also operates between Ireland and the United Kingdom.

From time to time, countries in these various regions do impose tighter controls at individual borders, as a reflection of practical difficulties as well as occasional hostilities. For example, borders between Qatar and Saudi-Arabia were closed in 2017, and travel between Qatar and other members of the Gulf Cooperation Council became subject to constraints.

Schengen and beyond

The combined population of the 29 countries in the Schengen region is currently 421 million. Adding in the populations of Ireland and the United Kingdom would bring the total to 493 million, which is 6.4% of the global population of 7,714 million. Achieving an open border region comprising 25% of the world's population will therefore require significant additional growth and mergers. Like the other goals in this roadmap, it's a challenging vision, especially in the light of recent political changes in the UK, but it's one that is important to keep in mind.

Larger free travel areas, whilst providing additional liberties and enhanced opportunities, will in general also involve an acceptance by individual countries of giving up portions of their local sovereignty, with decisions on matters impacting the entire region being taken by consensus at a multinational level, rather than just at the national level. However, this kind of pooling of sovereignty should be evaluated, not just from the viewpoint of what an individual country appears to lose, but also from the viewpoint of the additional benefits of strength-in-depth.

Another important factor that will enable and encourage this kind of agreement on freer movement is when localities and countries around the world no longer experience seemingly "being left behind". Reduced regional and global inequality will reduce the powerful pressures that people feel to rush to relocate to areas of visibly greater prosperity and flourishing. Accordingly, various elements of RAFT 2035 address not only the creation of abundance but also the equitable circulation and distribution of that abundance, worldwide. Perhaps counter-intuitively, when there is less urgency about the need to migrate, it will enable a fuller and more productive set of migration.

The UK and the EU

The decision by the UK to leave the EU, taken in a national referendum in June 2016, and in effect re-confirmed in the General Election of December 2019, rules out the possibility of the UK remaining within the main EU framework. However, in the years ahead, a number of other changes are likely to take place:

- A restructuring of the EU into a number of different layers of membership and associate membership

- Extensions in the relationships between the EU and other nations (and groupings of nations) around the world
- An awareness within the UK of the importance of minimising unnecessary friction in the relationship between the UK and the countries in the EU
- An increased appreciation of the benefits of managed open borders, as envisioned by RAFT
- A growing acceptance that greater opportunities and greater liberty involves surrendering some elements of local autonomy – similar to how (as described by Thomas Hobbes long ago[86]) the different citizens in a locale gain important new opportunities and liberties when they surrender some of their own autonomy to local government.

Accordingly, the position of the UK in a future enlarged version of Schengen may or may not involve the UK in due course formally rejoining the EU. That choice remains open.

Fear of culture overrun

One factor lies behind much of the apprehension about open borders. This fear goes beyond economic matters and focuses on culture change. The idea, expressed in, for example, the writings of Douglas Murray, is that:

- Western European culture has grown stale and feeble
- Western Europe is filled, not only with a panoply of trivialities, but also with loathing and self-doubt,

- In contrast, immigrant groups often bring a self-confident culture with them from overseas
- The culture of immigrant groups is often opposed to the norms and freedoms that Western Europe champions
- Especially when combined with particular strains of Islam, immigrant culture can give rise to murders, rapes, and terrorist outrages
- Even if second and third generation immigrants appear to have assimilated to Western European norms, they may flip back to extreme elements of their parents' culture, especially when experiencing alienation and emptiness.

In summary, to quote the first sentence of Murray's book *The Strange Death of Europe*[87],

> Europe is committing suicide.

One response to this analysis would be to argue for stronger barriers to entry, along with a revival of traditional Western European culture – particularly traditional Christianity with its formerly mighty network of churches and apparent moral certainties.

Never mind that the raw statistics of violence committed by immigrants can be queried – and that there is evidence that immigrants are, on the whole, more law-abiding than people with longer roots in a locale. The "suicide" argument resonates with some listeners on different levels of thinking, especially in times of economic distress. Because of feeling left behind by the pace of change, these listeners are quick to cast blame on people who seem alien – people who dress differently, eat different food, and appear to worship deities in different ways.

However, RAFT disagrees with this response. Rather than seeking a return to a bygone age of dominance of culture by Christian churches and traditional morality (with much reduced social diversity), here's a better response. It's a response that looks forwards rather than backwards:

- Elevate the RAFT vision of a near-term future with abundant flourishing for all
- Clarify which elements of diversity should indeed be restricted (in order to avoid destruction of human flourishing), and which, instead, should be supported and celebrated
- Make explicit a (short) list of elements of the local culture that need to be upheld as sacrosanct
- Highlight ways in which the aspirations of members of formerly dominant religions – aspirations for improved health, improved prosperity, improved wisdom, and an improved sense of meaning and purpose – can be met, not via a forced re-imposition of centuries-old beliefs and practices, but by the wise use of twenty first century science and technology.

Interim targets

To accelerate progress with Goal 8, two interim targets for 2025 are proposed:

1. Reach a general understanding of the economic case for open borders, and the types of constraints that need to be applied so that the benefits significantly outweigh the drawbacks.

2. Agree a statement of the "core values of all UK residents", highlighting those features of law and practice which are regarded as key to harmony and flourishing within the UK. This statement can also make it clear which elements of human and transhuman variation and diversity should be accepted or even encouraged – and which elements of diversity should be resisted. The UK's participation in an extended open border region can be made conditional upon ongoing compatibility of the UK's agreed core values with the corresponding practice throughout the wider region in question.

Moving forwards

An issue which is poised to put grave strain on international relations – and to generate huge waves of migrants that will stress tolerance to breaking points – is that of climate change. That's the subject of the next chapter.

For more information

- The 2017 book by Rutger Bregman, *Utopia for Realists: How We Can Build the Ideal World*[88]
- The 2018 book by Jonathan Portes, *What Do We Know and What Should We Do about Immigration?*[89]
- The 2011 book by Ian Goldin, *Exceptional People: How Migration Shaped Our World and Will Define Our Future*[90]
- Chapter 4, "Principles and priorities"[91], of the 2019 book by David Wood, *Sustainable Superabundance*[92]
- The 2019 book by Tony Czarnecki, *Democracy for a Human Federation: Coexisting with Superintelligence*[93].

9. Carbon neutrality

Goal 9 of RAFT 2035 is that **the UK will be carbon-neutral, thanks to improved green energy management.**

Unless countries all around the world become carbon-neutral, there are major risks of chaotic changes in global climate arising from runaway global warming. In turn, these chaotic changes in climate will cause chaotic adverse changes in human society.

All the other goals in this roadmap are vulnerable to becoming pointless if such a climate catastrophe occurs.

Avoidance of potential climate catastrophe will require strong international cooperation, but the solutions will be accelerated by bold actions of individual countries, such as the UK.

As individual countries take action, it will alter the set of motivations applicable to other countries. That's why it makes good sense for the UK to demonstrate leadership and to target carbon-neutrality more aggressively than the commitments made by some other countries.

Defining carbon neutrality

The phrase "carbon neutral" is shorthand for an overall neutral effect of all actions by a country that increase or decrease the likelihood of runaway global warming. These actions include all emissions of greenhouse gases from industry and from domestic use of energy, as well as processes to extract greenhouse gases from the atmosphere.

This goal explicitly rejects any reliance on "carbon offsetting", in which money is paid in some kind of compensation for greenhouse gas emissions. The reduction of greenhouse gases must be actual, rather than just conceptual.

This goal likewise rejects any creative accounting in which various actions initiated by the UK are completely omitted from the balance sheet – actions such as international shipping, flights to overseas destinations, and the production of goods overseas for import into the UK.

We cannot lower the risk of climate catastrophe by any such "greenwashing" measures of "sweeping data under the carpet". We need to assess the situation honestly and transparently. We also need to be ready to leave behind any ideological baggage that can prevent us from taking seriously the messages of the overwhelming majority of scientists who have studied this field.

The current trajectory

For a detailed discussion of measurement of overall "carbon footprint", including "consumption emissions", refer to the report published regularly by Defra, the UK's Department for Food and Rural Affairs, "UK's carbon footprint"[94]. From that report:

> In 2016 total greenhouse gas emissions associated with UK consumption were 3 per cent lower than in 1997 when this series [of measurements] begins.
>
> The UK's carbon footprint peaked in 2007 at 997 million tonnes CO2 equivalent. In 2016 it was 21 per cent lower than the 2007 peak (784 million tonnes CO2 equivalent).

A linear extrapolation of the trend from 2007 to 2016 would suggest that the UK could be carbon neutral within 36 years from 2016, namely 2052. The proposed goal evidently requires a considerable acceleration in the transformation to greener activities.

Note that this RAFT goal is fully compatible with people using large amounts of energy (and large amounts of resources). There's no intrinsic need to revert to a more frugal lifestyle. The point, instead, is to ensure that the energy avoids undue emissions of greenhouse gases (and that resources are replenished in a sustainable manner).

Exponential change

It has been known for more than a century how extra greenhouse gases can trap more of the sun's energy and raise average global temperatures. But the dynamic heat circulation mechanisms within the earth's overall climate systems are fiendishly complicated. Different experts make different forecasts about future impacts, and express different levels of confidence in these predictions.

Emphatically, this degree of uncertainty is no reason to dismiss concerns. As a matter of prudence, scenarios in which drastic changes could take place within just a few decades need to be taken very seriously.

These runaway scenarios feature adverse positive feedback cycles, the destabilisation of long-established current patterns in oceans or the atmosphere, and increased destruction from extreme weather events.

RAFT emphasises the drawbacks of linear thinking, and of the importance of adopting exponential thinking. This holds not just for potential increases in technological capability, but also for potential impacts from human activities on the environment. In particular, the threat of climate change goes beyond the possibility of mere linear changes in temperature. Increased heat could spark a comparatively sudden phase change in the earth's climate, pushing up the global average temperature by several degrees in less than a decade.

Similar sudden climate changes have taken place in the geological past, resulting in mass extinctions of large numbers of animal and plant species. These past changes had causes outside of any conscious choices by any of the animals involved. But this time, it will be different, due to the accumulated impact that human waste of all sorts is having on the planet. This time, the outcome *is* under conscious control – *provided* we humans pay sufficient collective attention.

Smaller calamities could prove disastrous in their own way, via what are known as "threat multiplier" mechanisms. The US Department of Defence warns of climate change[95] acting as a set of "threat multipliers that will aggravate stressors abroad such as poverty, environmental degradation, political instability, and social tensions – conditions that can enable terrorist activity and other forms of violence".

Social unrest that can (just about) be contained at the present time, may become completely unmanageable in the context of greater damage being inflicted regularly by extreme weather on agriculture, transport, and other key aspects of daily life. It is said that every society is only four square meals away from revolution and anarchy. That's not a theory we should be in any hurry to test.

Solutions and obstacles

The good news is that a number of technologies to comprehensively reduce the threat of damaging climate change are being developed and applied. The price of energy from wind, wave, and solar has been dropping steadily, decade after decade. New designs can improve capacity as well as drive down costs even further. As costs continue to fall, additional tipping points will be reached, enabling faster changes in adoption. After all, more than enough energy reaches the earth from the sun in just a few hours, to meet the needs of the entire human population for a whole year. In principle, all that's needed is to accelerate improvements in the harvesting, storage, and transmission of energy from renewable sources.

The bad news, however, is that the pace of implementing improvements is currently far too slow. It's not just that the generation of electricity needs to swap over from carbon-based to clean mechanisms. We also need widespread reforms of other economic activities that are collectively responsible for more than fifty percent of greenhouse gas emissions – activities such as farming, transport, and the manufacture of steel and cement. Another complication is a potential shortage of the raw materials needed in increasing quantities in the construction of ever larger numbers of solar panels, wind turbines, and other generators of clean energy.

Accordingly, political action to accelerate the transition is needed as a matter of the utmost priority.

This political action includes:

- Significant subsidies for next generation green technologies – including next generation systems for energy storage and energy transmission, as well as mechanisms such as "artificial photosynthesis" to create fuels from sunlight

- The steady reduction of subsidies (direct or indirect) for activities that increase greenhouse gas pollution – subsidies from which the oil and gas industry greatly benefits at present (although it works hard to keep these connections hidden)
- The imposition of taxes on activities that pollute – progressive taxes that scale up over time, with the revenues being distributed to the consumers most impacted by all these changes.

Together, these actions will increase the incentives favouring cleaner modes of operation.

Opposing forces

Political actions in support of carbon neutrality are facing trenchant opposition from the companies and organisations who perceive themselves as benefiting from the status quo. Oil corporations are among the most powerful on the planet, and they are backed by vigorous actions of the governments in countries where the oil industry is dominant.

Such opposition cannot be overcome by friendly rational persuasion alone. Other sorts of forces will need to be applied in parallel:

- Economic forces of subsidies and taxes

- Civil court cases suing for compensation for damage caused by extreme weather
- Legislative forces that support whistle blowers and legitimate protesters in the face of intimidation from vested interests
- A transformed, energised public mindset (this force may be the most important on the list).

On that last matter, it has been estimated[96] that the world faces an additional 30 trillion dollars in climate-related damages, depending on whether the globe remains on its present trajectory for 2 degrees Centigrade temperature rise (or worse), or whether actions are taken to keep temperature rises to the 1.5 degree goal agreed in Paris in 2015. Awareness of that level of additional cost deserves to change the public mindset. This awareness should also accelerate disinvestment in the oil corporations and other industries that will be increasingly held liable to cover the huge costs of this damage.

Action to tackle climate change also faces trenchant opposition from people who are ideologically opposed to any mechanisms for international collaboration, or to any intervention by the state to constrain the excesses of powerful corporations. These critics fear that such interventions or collaborations will inevitably be hugely heavy-handed, and will destroy innovation. However, a fuller review of history shows that such a fear is misplaced. On the contrary, if large corporations gain too much power, the needs of humanity as a whole would take a dismal second place.

This is a case where avoiding intervention would be deeply irresponsible. Positive, lean intervention is both possible and desirable.

Open minds

In order to obtain and maintain carbon neutrality, it will be important to keep an open mind about solutions worth exploring, and to be ready to transcend prior doctrinaire ideological positions.

Subject to careful review, vital roles could be played by innovations in:

- Nuclear fission and/or nuclear fusion
- Negative emissions technologies (carbon capture and storage)
- Various geoengineering initiatives.

If judged appropriate to proceed, these solutions will likely need significant political and financial support in order to progress sufficiently quickly.

Interim targets

To accelerate progress with Goal 9, two targets for 2025 are proposed (both targets overlap with the corresponding interim targets for Goal 4, that is, the abolition of homelessness and no involuntary hunger):

1. Agreement on a replacement for the GDP index as the guiding light for evaluating the success of the economy. The focus in this case is ensuring that the replacement for the GDP fully incorporates factors known as "externalities", that is the impacts of economic activities which are

presently excluded from valuations. Externalities can be positive as well as negative. Chief among negative externalities are adverse impacts on the environment.

2. Establish a reliable, respected source of information about the true environmental benefits and risks of different types of human actions. Existing highly contentious arguments about climate change scenarios should have the raw emotion and panic removed from them, so we can all see more clearly what are the real risks and real opportunities. In view of the passion that is manifest on all sides of the debate on climate change, and the deep suspicions about subterfuge, bad faith, and hidden motivations, this target will be challenging to achieve – which makes it all the more necessary.

Moving forwards

Climate change is only one of a number of very serious risks threatening the ability of the earth to continue to provide a positive environment for human activity. The next chapter looks more generally at the prospects of breaching "planetary boundaries".

For more information

- Chapter 5, "Towards abundant energy"[97], of the 2019 book by David Wood, *Sustainable Superabundance*[98]
- The edX MOOC from the University of Queensland, *Making Sense of Climate Science Denial*[99]
- The 2019 book by David Wallace-Wells, *The Uninhabitable Earth: Life After Warming*[100]

- The 2019 book by Rachel Maddow, *Blowout: Corrupted Democracy, Rogue State Russia, and the Richest, Most Destructive Industry on Earth*[101]
- The 2019 book by Matt Stoller, *Goliath: The 100-Year War Between Monopoly Power and Democracy*[102]
- The 2018 book by Varun Sivaram, *Taming the Sun: Innovations to Harness Solar Energy and Power the Planet*[103]
- The 2017 book by Peter Brannen, *The Ends of the World: Supervolcanoes, Lethal Oceans, and the Search for Past Apocalypses*[104]
- The 2014 book by Ramez Naam, *The Infinite Resource: The Power of Ideas on a Finite Planet*[105]
- The 2014 book by Naomi Klein, *This Changes Everything: Capitalism vs. The Climate*[106]
- The 2010 book by Naomi Oreskes, *Merchants of Doubt: How a Handful of Scientists Obscured the Truth on Issues from Tobacco Smoke to Global Warming*[107]

10. Zero waste

Goal 10 of RAFT 2035 is that **the UK will be zero waste, and will have no adverse impact on the environment**.

As human activity becomes more intense and more widespread, it often has unexpected adverse impacts on our environment. Goal 9 covered the particular case of runaway global warming, resulting from increased greenhouse gas emissions. Another example is that widespread pollution from plastics currently threatens numerous ecosystems around the world. Yet another example is the way that fracking for oil and gas increases the risk and magnitude of earthquakes.

Indeed, a number of so-called "planetary boundaries" are approaching dangerous tipping points. The ways in which we use resources from the environment need to be altered, onto a demonstrably *sustainable* basis. What this means is that *present-day flourishing cannot be at the expense of requiring a reduction in future flourishing.*

Without success with Goal 10, all bets are off, regarding achievement of any of the other RAFT goals.

However, by applying innovations in recycling, manufacturing, and waste management, the UK can become zero waste by 2035. As other countries around the world follow suit, the various dangers of environmental collapse can be avoided. Importantly, this can be achieved without requiring humans to adopt a diminished, restricted lifestyle. With a suitable framework in place, we can live in a world with a sustainable superabundance of material goods, healthy nutrition, frequent travel, high quality accommodation, and much more.

Planetary boundaries

Researchers from the Stockholm Resilience Centre, supported by partners around the world, have identified nine "planetary boundaries" where human activity is at risk of pushing the environment into potentially very dangerous states of affairs:

1. Climate change
2. Loss of biosphere integrity, that is, biodiversity loss and species extinctions
3. Stratospheric ozone depletion
4. Ocean acidification
5. Biogeochemical cycles (such as flows of nitrogen and phosphorus to the biosphere and oceans)
6. Land-system change (such as deforestation)
7. Freshwater consumption
8. Atmospheric aerosol loading, that is, microscopic particles in the atmosphere that affect climate and living organisms
9. Introduction of novel entities, such as organic pollutants, radioactive materials, nanomaterials, and microplastics.

As the researchers say:

> Crossing a boundary increases the risk that human activities could inadvertently drive the Earth System into a much less hospitable state, damaging efforts to reduce poverty, and leading to a deterioration of human wellbeing in many parts of the world, including wealthy countries.

The latest data indicates that four of the nine boundaries may have already been crossed: climate change, loss of biosphere integrity, land-system change, and altered biogeochemical cycles.

Complications and oversight

Whilst good solutions are at hand for each of the nine risks, we need to be aware of two important complications.

The first complication is that there may be unforeseen drawbacks from various technological interventions that are proposed as solutions to the threats of environmental collapse or resource shortage. In other words, the solutions may turn out to be worse than the problems they are trying to solve.

For example, there are reasons to fear potential unwelcome sweeping side-effects from agriculture or any other industry becoming overly dependent on new chemical treatments or new genetic manipulations. Larger and more mechanised doesn't necessarily mean more resilient. Biochemical or geoengineering innovations could have escalating adverse real-world consequences that weren't evident from short-term trials or localised pilots. The real world is a much messier, more complex place than any carefully controlled research laboratory.

This risk of unexpected escalating side-effects requires a total of four responses, as part of a proactive *RAFT oversight system*:

1. Proposed interventions must be widely discussed and analysed in advance, drawing upon insights from multiple disciplines and diverse perspectives.

2. Once interventions have been approved and applied, careful monitoring needs to take place, checking for any behaviours that differ from what was expected.
3. If any problems do come to light, swift reversals or other modifications will be required – hence the importance of governance that is both lean and agile.
4. Finally, a spirit of openness and transparency is vital, valuing data over ideology, transcending tribal instincts, and avoiding any temptations to ignore or obscure potential problems.

This brings us to the second complication: the various pressures which elevate short-term, group-specific perspectives over the full picture.

Consider the two-edged role that can be played by powerful corporations. Pursuit of profits often results in innovations that are profoundly useful. But just because a product makes good short-term financial sense for a company and its investors, that's no guarantee of a positive long-term effect on human well-being. For example, there are reasons to fear that the pursuit of profits by powerful agrochemical corporations could result, not in the feeding of the world, as promised by these corporations, but in a kind of unintentional poisoning of the world. Various industries have, alas, a long track record of seeking to cover up the risks associated with their products.

In summary, potential innovative solutions to environmental collapse or resource shortage face:

- The complication of multiple interactions, system issues, and unforeseen side-effects

- The complication of short-termism, blind group loyalty, and ideology trumping data.

These two sets of complications can be countered by proactive RAFT oversight, including the following:

- Ongoing systems analysis
- Trustable monitoring – as already described for goals 6 and 7
- Governance that is lean and agile
- Constraints on powerful sub-groups.

A key role will also be played by the uplifting RAFT vision of an abundance in which all sub-groups can flourish – an abundance with plenty for everyone.

Overcoming inertia

Despite the complications described above, there are positive routes ahead for each of the nine planetary boundaries identified, as well as for other possible impending environmental crises. The same themes emerge in each case:

- Methods are known, in outline at least, that would replace present unsustainable practices with sustainable ones
- By following these methods, life would be plentiful for all, without detracting in any way from the potential for ongoing flourishing in the longer term
- However, the transition from unsustainable to sustainable practices requires overcoming very significant inertia in existing systems

- In some cases, what's also required is vigorous research and development, to turn ideas for new solutions into practical realities
- Unfortunately, in the absence of short-term business cases, this research and development often fails to receive the investment it requires.

For each planetary boundary, the answers also follow the same pattern:

- Society as a whole needs to prioritise research and development of various potential solutions
- Society as a whole needs to agree on penalties and taxes that should be applied to increasingly discourage unsustainable practices
- Society as a whole needs to provide a social safety net to assist the people whose livelihoods are negatively impacted by these changes.

Left to its own devices, the free market is unlikely to reach the same conclusions. Instead, because it fails to assign proper values to various externalities, the market will produce harmful results. Accordingly, these are cases when society as a whole needs to constrain and steer the operation of the free market. In other words, democratic politics needs to assert itself.

Options to manage scarcity

In more detail, we can point to seven answers for how society can address scarcity of goods, without adversely impacting the environment:

1. Improvements in recycling processes – including greater use of nanotechnology – will be able to extract scarce materials from older products,

enabling higher amounts of re-use in newer products.

2. Alternative designs can be devised – often taking advantage of insights from artificial intelligence – that allow readily available materials to be used in place of rarer ones. In many cases, innovative new nanomaterials could serve as better alternatives to the components presently used.
3. As a consequence of better design and better manufacturing, material goods will become more robust, with self-cleaning and self-healing properties. This will extend their lifetimes, and reduce the need for rapid turnover of new products.
4. 3D printing can be used to manufacture goods that are precisely tailored to individual needs, at the point of need, and at the time of need, thereby reducing the wastage of surplus manufacture and unnecessary transport.
5. The asteroid belt, which mainly lies between the orbits of Mars and Jupiter, is thought to hold huge quantities of all sorts of elements. It will require a major project to mine these asteroids and transfer minerals back to the earth. However, by taking advantage of abundant solar energy, and with both spacecraft and mining equipment operated via automation, this project could make good economic sense.
6. Where there is a genuine scarcity, items should be shared, rather than being restricted to just a few owners. Accordingly, we should welcome the

growth of the circular economy, and the associated changes in public mindset.

7. The relative importance of material goods will in any case decline, as people come to value experiences more than possessions, and to spend greater amounts of their time in inner, virtual worlds.

It remains to be seen which of these seven answers will turn out to be more important in practice. What is clear is that there are many options to be explored. This exploration urgently needs higher priority and more focus.

Interim targets

To accelerate progress with Goal 10, two interim targets for 2025 are proposed (these targets are essentially the same as for Goal 9):

1. Agreement on a replacement for the GDP index as the guiding light for evaluating the success of the economy, where the replacement for the GDP fully incorporates all externalities (especially impacts on the environment).
2. Establish a reliable, respected source of information about the true environmental benefits and risks of different types of human actions. Existing highly contentious arguments about science and about environmental interactions should have the raw emotion and panic removed from them, so we can all see more clearly what are the real risks and real opportunities.

Moving forwards

An important particular example of the way humanity has transformed the environment is with enormous areas of farmland being dedicated to the raising and feeding of animals to be slaughtered to produce meat for human consumption. The next chapter foresees radical changes in this system.

For more information

- The 2019 book by Andrew McAfee, *More from Less: The Surprising Story of How We Learned to Prosper Using Fewer Resources—and What Happens Next*[108]
- The 2017 book by Kate Raworth, *Doughnut Economics: Seven Ways to Think Like a 21st-Century Economist*[109]
- Research by the Stockholm Resilience Centre on the nine planetary boundaries[110]

11. Clean meat

Goal 11 of RAFT 2035 is that **consumption of meat from slaughtered animals will be cut by at least 90%.**

Substitutes for meat from slaughtered animals include classical vegetarian diets, plant-based meat alternatives with broadly similar taste and texture as meat, and what is known as "clean meat", which is meat grown in laboratories from cultured cells using methods of biochemical engineering and synthetic biology.

Compared to existing meat sources, clean meat can, well before 2035, be healthier, tastier, better for the environment – by freeing up huge areas of land for other purposes – and can avoid the current situation of the mass slaughter of beings who possess at least some of the same characteristics of consciousness as humans.

Anticipating a change in public attitude

As technology provides a wider range of attractive substitutes, we can anticipate a growing change in public attitude. The writer Arwa Mahdawi has suggested that "Carnivores are going the way of cigarette smokers"[111]:

> By 2050, there's a good chance that it will be socially unacceptable to eat meat. In the same way that we're now horrified people used to smoke in offices and airplanes, we'll find it almost unthinkable that people used to consume animals so casually and frequently.

RAFT anticipates that this change in attitude could take place faster – well before 2050.

Plant-based meat alternatives

Plant-based meat alternatives are already growing in number. They include products from, in no particular order:

- Vivera – who state they are "Feeding the Goodness Revolution with the most delicious plant-based food"
- The Fry Family Food Co – who encourage consumers to "Swap meat with 100% plant-based products"
- Tofurky, with their plant-based burgers that are said to be not only "mouth-watering" but also "crazy good for the environment"
- Oumph – who claim their products have a "completely unique structure and texture... unlike anything else from the plant kingdom".

Other companies whose products contain plant-based meat alternatives, and which make broadly similar claims, include Linda McCartney Foods, Quorn, Gosh, Naturli, Iceland, Beyond Meat, Kellogg's Incogmeato, and Impossible Foods – the creators of the "Impossible Burger" served in some Burger King restaurants.

However, these products, along with lab-grown clean meat, presently face a number of challenges:

- Their taste and texture are felt by many to compare poorly to that of "real" meat
- The cost of lab-grown clean meat remains high
- There are no processes in place, yet, for larger-scale production of lab-grown meat.

More benefits ahead

Considerable research and development is now underway to address the challenges faced by clean meat. A report from the Adam Smith Institute, "The prospects for lab-grown meat"[112], urged UK businesses to increase investment in the field. The report highlighted progress in recent years as follows:

- In 2013 the cost of a burger made with meat grown in a lab stood at around $250,000, but by 2018, the price tag had dropped to just £8.
- Clean meat could mean a cut in agricultural greenhouse gas emissions of 78%-96%, while using 99% less land.
- Clean meat has the potential to solve the looming antibiotic resistance crisis. With farming using up to 70% of antibiotics critical to medical use in humans, cases of resistance are on the rise, driven by intensive farming practices.
- Clean meat will also reduce cases of food poisoning as, unlike on farms, growth takes place under controlled conditions.

Moreover, it is estimated that the processes that create clean meat will use 96% less freshwater, as well as 99% less land. (The meat portion of a single quarter pounder hamburger currently requires more than 2,000 litres of freshwater.)

Health benefits should also be emphasised: Since clean meat is grown in a sterile environment, there's no need to use antibiotics. Moreover, the levels of various types of cholesterol and fat in clean meat can be precisely controlled.

Think how much faster these important gains for the environment and for health could be realised if there is extra investment, not just from businesses, but also from the public sector.

Agricultural research already receives a sizeable budget from public funds. A significant portion of this budget should be applied to accelerating all aspects of progress with clean meat.

Making clean meat *really* clean

One complication with creating clean meat is the current reliance on one or more products that still need to be derived from slaughtered animals. These products include foetal bovine serum, a mixture harvested from the blood of foetuses excised from pregnant cows slaughtered in the dairy or meat industries. This serum contains a cocktail of proteins that make it well suited for helping all kinds of animal cells grow and duplicate.

Options to avoid use of foetal bovine serum include recombinant DNA technology and the use of pluripotent stem cells. The latter method has been adopted by the Dutch company Meatable, who have been working with researchers from Cambridge University.

As well as technical challenges to be overcome, there is the challenge of developing clean meat regulatory regimes that are suitably agile (that is, fast-moving), but also suitably robust. These regulatory systems need to guard against inadvertent public health risks, whilst avoiding becoming bogged down in any protectionist measures that give undue preference to the incumbent food production industry.

Critically, the public must be kept well-informed throughout, to prevent any emotion-charged panics similar to those over GMO foods.

Managing the transition

There are many potential new uses for the agricultural land that was formerly dedicated to livestock for the food industry. These uses include:

- New towns and cities
- Smart rural communities
- Regions for sports and other recreation
- Different forms of "rewilding" (as advocated by George Monbiot[113])
- Areas dedicated to "compassionate biology" (also known as "high-tech Jainism" or "paradise engineering").

Decisions on new usage should be taken, based not just on financial criteria, but taking into account the full range of flourishing covered in RAFT.

Inevitably, the changes envisioned in this goal will raise concerns for people who are presently employed in farming and in food processing. As with all RAFT projects, consideration should be given to putting in place subsidies and other assistance, to avoid unnecessary hardship during the transition.

Interim targets

To accelerate progress with Goal 11, two interim targets for 2025 are proposed:

1. Clarify the range of health benefits from alternatives to slaughtered meat, bearing in mind

that consumption of meat has been linked to many diseases.

2. Demonstrate "full taste parity" of selected alternatives to slaughtered meat.

In parallel, the rich variety of new types of meat that could soon become available – for example, meat equivalent to that from a stegosaurus or a tyrannosaurus – could stimulate much greater public interest in eating this sort of food.

Moving forwards

Humanity's longer-term future lies, not just on the Earth – with a much improved environment – but also in the universe beyond our home planet. The next chapter envisions a potential step-up in progress in our cosmic journey upwards and outwards.

For more information

- The 2018 book by Paul Shapiro, *Clean Meat: How Growing Meat Without Animals Will Revolutionize Dinner and the World*[114]
- The 2016 essay by David Pearce, *Compassionate Biology*[115]
- Meatable[116]
- Research by Peta UK: *Vegan Meat Brands That Are Changing Everything*[117]

12. Humanity on Mars

Goal 12 of RAFT 2035 is that **the UK will be part of an organisation that maintains a continuous human presence on Mars**.

A continuous human presence on Mars will help transform humanity's perspective, from being inward-looking and Earth-bound, to being outward-looking and cosmos-embracing.

As an alternative, robot exploration of Mars could carry out many useful scientific experiments, but having humans present there too will provide a significant additional perspective. A round trip visit to Mars by robots can act as an important prelude to a round trip visit by humans.

Journeys to Mars can also provide useful information and experience that will assist subsequent trips to the asteroid belt, with the possibility of mining the asteroids, as mentioned in the discussion of Goal 10.

Raising consciousness

When astronauts reached the Moon in the late 1960s, it raised the consciousness of people all over the Earth who avidly watched the adventure on TV screens. Conflicts between different nations were forgotten, for a while at least. The astronauts carried an American flag, but could also be seen as representatives of the entire planet.

The "earthrise" photograph, taken by astronaut Bill Anders while orbiting the moon in Apollo 8 on Christmas Eve 1968, helped ignite a worldwide grassroots "whole earth" movement. Anders observed, "We came all this way to explore the Moon, and the most important thing is that we discovered the Earth".

Reflecting on the perspective provided from the windows of Apollo 8, American poet Archibald MacLeish wrote these words in the New York Times[118]:

> To see the Earth as it truly is, small and blue and beautiful in that eternal silence where it floats, is to see ourselves as riders on the Earth together, brothers on that bright loveliness in the eternal cold – brothers who know now they are truly brothers.

Rusty Schweickart, an astronaut on the next flight in the same series, Apollo 9, undertook a space walk as part of that trip. For five minutes he simply stared at the Earth below him. He later summarised his thoughts as follows[119]:

> You look down there and you can't imagine how many borders and boundaries you cross, again and again and again, and you don't even see them. There you are – hundreds of people in the Middle East killing each other over some imaginary line that you're not even aware of, that you can't see. And from where you see it, the thing is a whole, the earth is a whole, and it's so beautiful. You wish you could take a person in each hand, one from each side in the various conflicts, and say, "Look. Look at it from this perspective. Look at that. What's important?"

Changes in focus

Back in the 1970s, it was widely assumed that humans would visit Mars before the end of the century. However, in the years that followed, Nasa's interest was diverted instead onto an international space station, which produced its own line of benefits – including learning how astronauts can spend ever longer periods of time away from the Earth.

It has been independent entrepreneurs such as Elon Musk and Jeff Bezos that have, more recently, rekindled the idea of interplanetary travel, making impressive progress with their companies SpaceX and Blue Origin.

What is needed now is productive collaboration between the best elements of public and private initiatives. Moreover, the project will benefit significantly from input from around the world, including resources in the UK.

One important field of innovation could be in new types of rocket, that would reduce the amount of time required to travel between the Earth and Mars. As summarised by a BBC review article "New engine tech that could get us to Mars faster"[120], alternative engine mechanisms potentially include:

- Solar electric propulsion
- Nuclear thermal electric propulsion
- Electric ion propulsion.

Interim targets

To accelerate progress with Goal 12, two interim targets for 2025 are proposed:

1. Humans will walk on the Moon again, helping humanity to rediscover a sense of cosmic delight. These new visitors to our nearest cosmic neighbour should include women as well as men, and people from many different nationalities.

2. A round trip mission to Mars will be underway, using robots, to collect rock samples and then return them to Earth.

Expertise from the United Kingdom can assist both of these projects.

Moving forwards

Humanity's journey into the wider cosmos involves, not just physical movement, but gradual mastery of the most powerful energy sources of the cosmos. This includes taming the enormous energy of nuclear fusion – the subject of the next chapter.

For more information

- An IDA (Institute for Defence Analyses) assessment, *Evaluation of a Human Mission to Mars by 2033*[121]
- The Earthrise photo[122]
- "Earth from the Moon"[123] photo montage
- The Mars Society[124]
- The 2017 documentary film about the two Voyager spacecraft, *The Farthest*[125]
- The 2019 book by Robert Zubrin, *The Case for Space: How the Revolution in Spaceflight Opens Up a Future of Limitless Possibility*[126]

13. Nuclear fusion

Goal 13 of RAFT 2035 is that **fusion (the energy source of the stars) will be generating at least 1% of the energy used in the UK**.

Nuclear fusion has the potential to provide vast amounts of safe, clean energy, once we have solved the deep technical and collaboration issues that have held up implementation so far.

First conceived as a theoretical possibility in the 1920s by the British physicists Francis Aston and Arthur Eddington, nuclear fusion has regularly been said since the 1940s to be "thirty years in the future". Containing hydrogen at temperatures over 100 million degrees Centigrade in a fusion reactor poses numerous engineering difficulties.

However, if these problems could be solved, fusion will have many benefits:

- Enormous fuel supplies
- Little waste product
- Low, easily manageable quantities of radioactivity.

To give a comparison: whereas the UK economy uses each day the energy from several supertankers full of oil, less than one thousandth of a single supertanker containing fuel for nuclear fusion – namely isotopes of hydrogen – would provide enough energy to run the UK economy for an entire year.

ITER – ambitious but slow

The largest fusion development project underway is ITER, which stands for "International Thermonuclear Experimental Reactor". It is one of the world's most ambitious long-term collaborative engineering projects.

Joint US-Soviet funding for ITER was agreed during talks between Ronald Reagan and Mikhail Gorbachev in 1985. As of 2005 the main funding has been split between seven parties, with the European Union contributing 45%, and six other countries contributing roughly 9% each: the US, China, Russia, India, Japan, and South Korea.

Construction of the main ITER complex started in 2013, in Saint Paul-lez-Durance, southern France. Construction is scheduled to complete in 2025, with full scale experiments expected by 2035.

Given the lengthy timescales involved, and a history of budget overruns, questions are frequently raised about the viability of the project. These questions often focus on political matters of how the collaboration will proceed, rather than questions of science or engineering.

Some alternative approaches

In parallel with ITER, a number of smaller-scale nuclear fusion research projects have been seeking funding from different sources, including venture capitalists. Being smaller and nimbler, these projects are more open to adopting disruptive innovative ideas.

These projects include:

- The SPARC (SPherical Affordable Robust Compact) reactor at MIT, whose website describes an "overall strategy of speeding up fusion development by using new high-field, high-temperature superconducting (HTS) magnets"

- The Tokamak Energy project in Milton, Oxfordshire in the UK, whose website envisions "industrial scale energy with the 'Fusion Power Demonstrator' by 2025" and "clean and abundant fusion power by 2030"
- First Light Fusion, also based in Oxfordshire, which states that it is "pursuing pulsed power driver technology, which we believe will reduce costs by an order of magnitude" – and that it "plans to demonstrate gain – generating more energy than that required to create fusion reactions – by 2024" (no fusion project anywhere in the world has yet managed to demonstrate gain).

Options for faster progress

The long timescales of nuclear fusion projects – even the ones which have aspirations to proceed more quickly – mean they experience difficulty in attracting sufficient private funding. Accordingly, substantial progress may depend upon more public funding being made available.

However, one factor which could accelerate progress is the application of improved artificial intelligence systems:

- To review and propose the design of nuclear fusion systems
- To direct plasma stabilisation and containment in real-time.

Another source of potential breakthrough – admittedly less likely, but still worth considering – is that new quantum computing systems might enable more effective modelling of some of the interactions involved inside fusion reactions.

Interim targets

To accelerate progress with Goal 13, two targets for 2025 are proposed:

1. Complete the construction of ITER facilities, as per its current committed schedule, without any further delays.
2. At least one smaller fusion project will make tangible progress, leading as a result to greater public enthusiasm about the feasibility of successful fusion energy being available by 2035.

Moving forwards

Progress with each of the RAFT goals depends on positive action from political leaders. However, political leaders have a miserably low reputation in the current time. The next chapter addresses how that fact can change, and how politics can become more effective and productive.

For more information

- ITER "unlimited energy"[127]
- MIT Sparc[128]
- Tokamak Energy[129]
- First Light Fusion[130]
- Financial Times review article *Two British companies confident of nuclear fusion breakthrough*[131]

14. Politicians and trust

Goal 14 of RAFT 2035 is that **politicians will no longer act in ways that are self-serving, untrustworthy, or incompetent.**

As a result of progress towards this goal, members of the general public will hold politicians in much higher regard and respect.

This is the first in a group of two goals in the sector of significantly improved political flourishing. With progress towards both of these goals, society will increasingly be guided by the best of human insight, in close, productive collaboration with the best of AI insight.

Politicians mistrusted and disliked

Given the key role of politics in progressing the other goals set out in this roadmap, it's a major drawback that there is as much mistrust and dislike of politicians as is presently the case in the UK. Instead of encouraging and enabling collaboration between multiple different groups of talent and insight in the country, our politicians are creating more division and more hard-heartedness.

The 2019 Ipsos MORI "Veracity Index" poll[132] measured the level of esteem attributed to a variety of professions by members of the British public. Respondents to the survey were asked if they generally trusted people from specified professions to tell the truth.

Politicians came at the very bottom of the list, with a positive rating of only 14%. This is worse than, for example, advertising executives (17%), journalists (26%), estate agents (30%), business leaders (35%), and bankers (43%). For comparison, the profession of nurses came out best, with a positive rating of 95%, followed by doctors on 93%, and teachers on 89%.

As a further indication of the dire state of the reputation of politicians in the UK, consider the Edelman "Trust Barometer" findings for 2019[133]. This contains the following evaluations by members of the public of various traits of politicians in the UK:

- "Honest with the public" – judged as a most important trait by 72% of respondents, but 58% said that "few/none of the UK's political leaders show this trait"
- "A good communicator" – judged as a most important trait by 64% of respondents, but 38% said that "few/none of the UK's political leaders show this trait".

Positive roles for politicians

However, there's nothing inevitable about politicians being held in such poor regard. The European Social Survey[134] regularly evaluates the level of trust in politicians in 32 countries in and around Europe. The UK generally ranks about 12th best in this survey – well ahead of countries such as Poland, Portugal, Ukraine, Croatia, and Bulgaria, but significantly behind Denmark (the top of the list), Switzerland, Netherlands, Luxembourg, Norway, Finland, Sweden, and Iceland.

Let's remember the vital role that politicians can play in society: to deliberate, speak, and act on behalf of all citizens, protecting the community from exploitation by members of powerful subgroups. Politicians establish and then regularly review the operation of laws – laws whereby members of society collectively agree to give up various potential freedoms, and to accept specific responsibilities, in order that society gains overall – with greater individual flourishing too. In this vision, to be a politician is to be a servant of the community.

In times of faster change in technology and social structures, wise political action becomes even more important. This will require politicians who can absorb new information, incorporate the latest insights from multiple fields of knowledge, update their worldviews, and revise legal and political systems speedily and precisely. In short, it will require a new calibre of politician, able to take advantage of the best understanding that becomes available, rather than sticking to the slogans that have gained them some personal popularity in the past.

Improving trust and respect

Measures that can increase the level of trust and respect for politicians include:

- Increased transparency, to counter any suspicions of hidden motivations or vested interests
- Automated real-time objective fact-checking, so that politicians know any distortions of the truth will be quickly pointed out
- The calculation and publication of "reliability indexes" for individual politicians, based on the quality of their words and deeds, as evaluated against agreed criteria

- Encouragement of individual politicians with high ethical standards and integrity
- Enforcement of penalties in any cases where politicians knowingly create or pass on false information
- Easier mechanisms for the electorate to be able to quickly "recall" a politician when they have lost the trust of voters
- Improvements in mental health for everyone (as covered in Goal 2), including politicians, thereby diminishing tendencies for dysfunctional behaviour
- Regular psychometric assessment of politicians, to highlight warning signs early
- Diminished power for political parties to constrain how individual politicians express themselves, allowing more politicians to speak according to their own true conscience
- Changes in the voting system, to enable and encourage electors to vote for the candidates they most admire, rather than feeling obliged to vote tactically.

Improving the voting system

The proposed change in the voting system will move beyond the present outdated "first past the post" voting system. Under this present system, voters frequently feel unable to vote for the candidate that most matches their own outlooks. They fear that such a vote would have the undesired side-effect of letting a deeply disliked candidate win the election. Accordingly, they vote instead for the candidate they perceive as "the least worst, of those who have a real chance of winning the election."

However, under a system of ranked transferable votes, voters could indicate not only their first choice, but also a complete ranking of the other candidates. This change will allow more authentic voting.

In parallel with the adoption of ranked transferable votes, a revision from single-MP constituencies to larger multi-MP regional constituencies, similar to those already used for EU elections, will address the current overly-high barriers of entry being faced by new parties. As a result, it will enable more fluid changes within the set of political parties.

Here are some important consequences of these changes in the political system:

1. Politicians will need to become better at working in coalitions and alliances with people from different parties. Of course, that's a good skill to develop!
2. Politicians will have to demonstrate their own individual qualities, rather than expecting to coast into parliament merely by belonging to a popular party.
3. The power of big finance to control politicians should diminish, as individual politicians can take advantage of technology to communicate their messages to the electorate at low cost but high fidelity.
4. The pace of political change should increase, allowing regulations and incentives (such as subsidies) to update quickly in line with fast changes in the worlds of technology and business.

Positive examples of system change

The task of changing the electoral system faces a challenge. The parties that fare badly under the current system (and which likely have the biggest motivation to support a change in the system) are those that failed to win the election; therefore they lack the power to put that change in place. Conversely, the parties that did win the election have less motivation to make such a change.

However, we should remember that:

- Even under the first past the post system, governments sometimes consist of coalitions – as in the UK from 2010 to 2015. Minority parties can make their support of such a coalition conditional upon legislation being brought forwards to reform elections.
- Many countries serve as examples of where first past the post was formerly used, but was subsequently rejected. This list[135] includes Australia, Belgium, Denmark, Lebanon, Malta, Mexico, Netherlands, New Zealand, Portugal, and South Africa.

Interim targets

To accelerate progress with Goal 14, two interim targets for 2025 are proposed:

1. Obtain majority public support for the design of a system to replace first past the post election – a new system that would eliminate a cause of a great deal of the ambivalence and hostility people feel towards their MPs. This step will, moreover,

establish the groundwork for the other changes described earlier.

2. Agree an understanding of the actual purpose of politicians, including the key role of the public sector in a mixed economy. This understanding will also include awareness of the role of industrial strategy – a concept that has often been unfairly maligned. Indeed, effective industrial strategy is vital to the success of many of the other goals in this roadmap.

Moving forwards

Beyond the improvements in politics resulting from this goal, the next chapter anticipates further changes in the capability and trustworthiness of politics, from wider use of AI and other decision support tools.

For more information

- Chapter 10, "Democracy and inclusion"[136], of the 2017 book by David Wood, *Transcending Politics*[137]
- The Electoral Reform Society[138]
- The 2012 book by Daron Acemoğlu and James Robinson, *Why Nations Fail: The Origins of Power, Prosperity, and Poverty*[139]
- The 2016 book by Jacob S. Hacker and Paul Pierson, *American Amnesia: Business, Government, and the Forgotten Roots of Our Prosperity*[140]
- The 2018 book by Oliver Bullough, *Moneyland: Why Thieves and Crooks Now Rule the World and How To Take It Back*[141]
- A reliability index for politicians?[142]

15. Politics and AI

Goal 15 of RAFT 2035 is that **parliament will involve a close partnership with a "House of AI" (or similar) revising chamber**.

To restate the goal: politics will benefit from a close positive partnership with enhanced Artificial Intelligence.

Politics features both the strengths and the weaknesses of humans, writ large. When we sometimes complain that our politicians are stupid or selfish, we should remember that humans in general can be stupid and selfish – as well as, on occasion, being wise and selfless. The difference is in the degree of power that politicians can possess.

The dangers of power

Power tends to corrupt, warned Lord Acton[143], the nineteenth century historian and politician. Absolute power corrupts absolutely. Power can corrupt the clarity of a politician's thinking, and their sense of moral duty. It can lead them to forget their social ties to their fellow citizens. It can cause them to *imagine themselves* as being particularly worthy and deserving. It's little wonder that initially admirable politicians often go downhill over time.

If power tends to corrupt, what is truly worrying is that never before have we humans held so much power in our hands. Science and technology are providing us with spectacular capabilities. We face the threat of unprecedented large scale surveillance and manipulation by forces seeking undue influence. This manipulation can be subtle rather than blatant. That's what gives it greater power. New technology also strengthens those who would wield fake news and other black-art psychological techniques to frighten or incite people into making choices that are different from their actual best interests. All this raises the spectre of politicians taking and holding power more vigorously than ever before.

Checks and balances, under threat

In principle, what limits politicians from abusing power is the set of checks and balances of a democratic society: separation of powers, a free press, independent courts, and regular elections. The effectiveness of elections depends, however, on electors being able to see matters sufficiently clearly, and to assess scenarios objectively.

Too often, alas, we electors prefer to mislead ourselves into believing comforting untruths and half-truths. We prefer reassuring slogans over an awareness that matters are actually much more complicated in reality. We use our intelligence, not to find out what is the true situation, but to find rationales that justify whatever we have already decided we want to do. We tend not to care much whether these rationales and slogans are sound. We care more that these slogans bolster our self-image, and raise our perceived importance inside the groups of people with whom we seek to identify. That's because we are, thanks to human nature, motivated too often by fear and by vanity.

Clever social media communications seek to push us into emotional reactions rather than careful deliberation. With our hearts on fire, smoke gets in our eyes. With our emotions inflamed, online interactions frequently propel us to champion tribal instincts. With a heightened sense of the importance of group identity, we cheer on pro-group "blue lies" rather than respecting objective analysis[144]. Afraid of having to admit we were previously mistaken, we double down on our convictions, in effect throwing good money after bad. We may succeed in ignoring reality – for a while, until reality bites back, with a vengeance.

Two sets of tools are available to prevent us continuing to misuse our individual human intelligences:

1. Collective intelligence, where people help each other to reason more thoughtfully
2. Artificial intelligence, with automated reasoning and data analysis.

Both these sets of tools will be deeply important in the years ahead. The tools interact, raising possibilities for faster progress. At the same time, we need to be aware that these tools are, in their own way, capable of bad outcomes too:

- Collective intelligence can produce collective stupidity
- AI can help people and corporations pursue dangerous goals more quickly than ever before.

We'll need to keep our wits about us!

The rise of AI

AI systems are quickly increasing in use around the world as decision support tools. For example, they provide support for medical decisions, legal reviews, assessment of credit worthiness, identifying the most suitable candidates for employment, and suggesting new partners for romance and intimacy. Software tools can highlight mistakes in spelling and grammar, awkwardness in style, and wording that is more likely to be effective for particular audiences.

Software tools can also flag up instances of mistaken facts, questionable sourcing, and the likelihood that some material, such as a video, has been fabricated or manipulated from its original content.

Before long, AI and other decision support tools should be able to provide very useful analysis and validation of political statements, including legislative changes that politicians are proposing. AI could identify potential problems with legislation sooner, and suggest creative new adaptations and syntheses of earlier ideas. AI can also alert us when we are becoming tired, bigoted, or selective in our use of evidence, and can recommend more fruitful ways to continue a discussion. This AI, therefore, could help us to become, not only cleverer, but also kinder and more considerate.

However, AI systems are prone to various amounts of bias, misunderstanding, quirks, and other faults – some of which are very serious. People who use these tools sometimes put too much trust in them, without independently assessing their recommendations. Another risk, identified by writer Jamie Bartlett as "the moral singularity", is that people will lose their ability to take independent hard decisions, through lack of practice, on account of delegating more and more decisions to AI systems. With atrophied moral intuitions, people will unintentionally become dominated by the moral decisions made on their behalf by machine intelligence. In short, there are many potential pitfalls ahead!

Accordingly, this RAFT goal seeks to obtain significant benefits of AI decision-making, whilst managing the significant risks of mistakes from these systems, and the risks if these systems are configured to serve the needs of only a small subset of human society.

There is no suggestion that AIs will have overall control of key decisions. Instead, what is envisioned is a productive partnership between human intelligence and machine intelligence, in which the final decision rests with human politicians.

The House of AI

The relationship between human politicians and the envisioned "House of AI" would follow the existing model between the House of Commons and the House of Lords: the Lords can revise and amend legislation originating in the Commons, but the Commons has the ability to override recommendations from the Lords.

What's more, just as the Commons can at present take account of ideas from groups of Lords in formulating new legislation, human politicians will in the future take ideas from the House of AI into consideration when drafting new political measures. As a further step, the House of AI could create *a menu of different political options*, along with an assessment of the pros and cons of each option, for human politicians to take the final decision.

Compared to the present processes, the result with the House of AI involved should be better political legislation, understood more widely, and passed into law considerably more quickly. It will be legislation that keeps up with the fast-changing issues raised by the latest social and technological developments.

For the House of AI to succeed, a number of points should be followed:

- All algorithms used by the House of AI will need to be in the public domain, and to pass ongoing reviews about their transparency and reliability
- Opaque algorithms, or other algorithms whose model of operation remains poorly understood, will need to be excluded, or evolved in ways addressing their shortcomings
- There will likely need to be public funding allocated to develop these systems, rather than us waiting for commercial companies to create them
- Indeed, the House of AI cannot be dependent on any systems owned or operated by commercial entities. Instead, it will be "AI of the people, by the people, for the people".

Interim targets

To accelerate progress with Goal 15, two interim targets for 2025 are proposed:

1. Reach an agreement on limits on the roles that can be played by commercially owned AI. This agreement should recognise the potential large contribution that could be made by commercially owned software, without being naive about the risks.
2. Reach an agreement on the principles of "ethical AI": what are the features which an AI *could* be built to include, but which will *need to be excluded or curtailed*, for the sake of true human flourishing?

These two agreements will both play a central role in the future evolution of RAFT. Different people and organisations have strongly divergent views about the scope and scale of such agreements. Obtaining consensus will require an honest and full consideration, not just of machine intelligence and machine goals, but also of human intelligence and human goals.

In other words, true progress is unlikely to be made with the question of "ethical AI" unless true progress is also made with the question of "ethical humanity".

We can hardly expect to obtain the best results from the machine intelligence of advanced software systems unless we figure out to obtain the best results from the different kind of "machine intelligence" that is displayed by the market system of profit-seeking corporations. Unless we know how to anticipate and remedy potential huge market failures, then what lies ahead will be huge AI failures – AI that serves, not the best aspects of humanity, but the worst aspects of humanity.

Moving forwards

Although the 15 goals of RAFT 2035 are wide-ranging, they omit some important ideas about future possibilities. The next chapter covers some of the concepts in this "bubbling under" category.

For more information

- The 2019 book by Rana Foroohar, *Don't Be Evil: How Big Tech Betrayed Its Founding Principles – and All of Us*[145]
- The 2019 book by Stuart Russell, *Human Compatible: Artificial Intelligence and the Problem of Control*[146]
- The 2019 book by Roger McNamee, *Zucked: Waking Up to the Facebook Catastrophe*[147]

- The 2019 book by Tom Chivers, *The AI Does Not Hate You: Superintelligence, Rationality and the Race to Save the World*[148]
- The 2018 book by Kevin Werbach, *The Blockchain and the New Architecture of Trust*[149]
- The 2018 book by Shoshana Zuboff, *The Age of Surveillance Capitalism: The Fight for a Human Future at the New Frontier of Power*[150]
- The 2018 book by Jamie Bartlett, *The People Vs Tech: How the Internet Is Killing Democracy (and How We Save It)*[151]
- The 2018 book by Jamie Susskind, *Future Politics: Living Together in a World Transformed by Tech*[152]
- The 2018 book by Thomas W. Malone, *Superminds: The Surprising Power of People and Computers Thinking Together*[153]

16. Bubbling under

RAFT is far from being a fixed and complete model. It is expected to grow and evolve in the months and years ahead.

As the ideas behind RAFT have been discussed ahead of publication, a number of other goals have been proposed for 2035, but have not yet been included in the main analysis. Borrowing a phrase[154] from publishers of charts of the most popular music tracks, these goals can be said to be "bubbling under": they fall below the present threshold for inclusion, but are sufficiently interesting to merit a short side-discussion.

Selected examples are listed below, with a view to versions of these goals potentially being adopted more widely in due course.

A charter for individual liberties?

RAFT emphasises social collaboration, with "no one being left behind" against their will. This includes what can be called a principle of "active neighbourliness": rather than keeping quiet about impending dangers about to befall someone, or major opportunities they are about to miss, we should find the way to speak up, just as we would ourselves like to be alerted to these dangers or opportunities in an equivalent circumstance.

At the same time, RAFT champions the fundamental importance of human individuality: *individual flourishing should not be sacrificed or subordinated to collectivist goals*. Society should protect and elevate all members of society.

Individuals should never become cannon-fodder in service of some tribal, national, ethnic, religious, or ideological quest.

Balancing the principles of human individuality and active neighbourliness can be challenging at times. Might a new charter of individual liberties help?

This charter would clarify reasons to uphold important rights, as well as reasons why people should accept important responsibilities and limits. The interplay of these points can be subtle.

Merely the fact that someone desires to carry out some kind of medical or lifestyle experiment, and claims to be fully informed about all the risks and consequences, cannot, by itself, convey the right to proceed. That's because the consequences of the experiment could extend beyond the person directly involved. Financial or social costs incurred by third parties could far exceed what these third parties expected.

However, *the positive upsides* to such an experiment could, likewise, exceed reasonable expectations. Therefore, care must be taken not to limit experimentation unnecessarily. Care is particularly required not to allow dominant subgroups to exert restrictive viewpoints over a community as a whole, obstructing innovation, where the effect of these restrictive viewpoints is to privilege existing power groups and to preserve the status quo.

In other words, there's a need to take into account, not only the direct effect of a medical or lifestyle (etc) experiment, but also what are called the "externalities" of that experiment. Failure to do so would be akin to commending a company whose profits depended on them hiding flows of waste pollution they are generating. Another comparison is with overlooking the "moral hazard" that arises from an otherwise commendable act of generosity or forgiveness.

Two terms that are heard in this discussion are "precautionary" and "proactionary". It is sometimes implied that a one-time choice must be made between these two poles. In reality, both principles are needed.

- The precautionary principle is appropriate when there are credible suggestions of huge negative consequences of some action. We need to beware unintended runaway consequences of well-meaning actions. This is particularly necessary when the distribution of outcomes has "long tails", in which extreme results will happen more frequently than under an assumption of the normal (Gaussian) distribution. An example of such a distribution is for the number of biological species that can become extinct over a given time period.
- The proactionary principle points out, on the other hand, that abstaining from action can have huge negative consequences as well. To adapt traditional language, there are "sins of omission" as well as "sins of commission". Rather than any blanket abstention from actions which have associated risks, it is often better to develop plans to manage these risks.

In many cases, a better principle than *precaution* is *reversibility*. Action that is risky should be undertaken in ways that allow reversal, in the event that matters develop badly.

Such a commitment to reversibility would require effective monitoring, and avoidance of any inertia that would overwhelm attempts to change course. It also requires the emotional intelligence that is willing to admit and experience failures, and to learn lessons from these failures.

The points mentioned could indeed be included in a charter of individual liberties, to be developed in the years ahead. Such work would dovetail with several of the interim goals already present in RAFT:

- Agreement on the basic elements of a revised social contract in which paid employment loses its prime position (from Goal 3)
- Establish a commitment from a majority of the countries in the United Nations to an updated version of the Universal Declaration of Human Rights, which takes fully into account the remarkable transformational nature of the technologies highlighted in RAFT (from Goal 7)
- Agree a statement of the "core values of all UK residents" (from Goal 8)
- Agreement on a replacement for the GDP index, that fully incorporates "externalities" (from Goals 9 and 10)
- Agree basic principles of the design and operation of systems for "trustable monitoring" (from Goal 6).

As well as seeking wide agreement on the *desirability* of various liberties, it's also important to develop products and services that makes these liberties *possible* and, indeed, *possible at scale.* That's the subject of the next two goals in this "bubbling under" list.

Cryonics suspension on the NHS?

Cryonics involves the body (or, in some cases, just the head, or the brain) being lowered to temperatures below minus 130 °C. At these temperatures, biological processes essentially cease. If someone has just been declared legally dead, cryonics prevents any further decomposition. The person may be legally dead, but is in principle capable of being revived at some later date, by which time the capabilities of medicine will be able to cure whatever disease or injury has brought their life to a pause.

Cryonics can be seen as providing a kind of "ambulance to the future" – a future time when bodies could be repaired or even reconstructed, allowing a fresh new lease of life. Cryonics will increase the chance of people being able to resume relationships with family and friends, to continue to develop their own skills, and to have more experiences. As such, cryonics can be seen as a potentially very powerful technology of liberation.

A group of 68 scientists have signed an open letter on cryonics[155], at various dates from 2004 onwards:

> To whom it may concern,
>
> Cryonics is a legitimate science-based endeavour that seeks to preserve human beings, especially the human brain, by the best technology available. Future technologies for resuscitation can be envisioned that involve molecular repair by nanomedicine, highly advanced computation, detailed control of cell growth, and tissue regeneration.

> With a view toward these developments, there is a credible possibility that cryonics performed under the best conditions achievable today can preserve sufficient neurological information to permit eventual restoration of a person to full health.
>
> The rights of people who choose cryonics are important, and should be respected.

Low temperature preservation is already in wide use for early-stage embryos, and for sperm and eggs. These have regained vitality when the temperature has been increased again. Simple organisms, such as the C. elegans worm, have been cryopreserved and then reanimated, and have demonstrated retention of memories of trained tasks at the end of the process[156].

However, the cost of cryonic suspension is currently upwards of $28,000 (via the American company Cryonics Institute[157]) or $80,000 (via another American company, Alcor[158]). These costs can rise higher to take care of standby costs, and, in the case of Alcor, further again, to $200,000, for the preservation of the whole body rather than just the head.

These high costs reflect the fact that very few people undergo the procedure at the present. Costs could come down significantly if benefits of scale can be achieved. Larger scale operation is also likely to improve the quality of the suspension, so there is less chance of damage being introduced.

The first person to be cryopreserved was Dr James Bedford, a 73-year old retired psychology professor. This took place on 12th January 1967. Despite the early cryonics community forecasting that the idea would soon become more popular, the rate of cryopreservation remains low to this day. For example, Alcor preserved[159] only 11 individuals in 2019, 10 in 2018, 5 in 2017, 6 in 2016, 10 in 2015, 13 in 2014, 7 in 2013, and 3 in 2012.

Indeed, there are currently many factors that discourage people from signing up for cryonics preservation. These include:

- Costs
- Problems arranging transport of the body overseas to a location where the storage of bodies is legal
- The perceived low likelihood of a subsequent successful reanimation
- Lack of evidence of reanimation of larger biological organs
- Dislike of appearing to be a "crank"
- Apprehension over tension from family members (exacerbated if family members expect to inherit funds that are instead allocated to cryopreservation services)
- Occasional mistrust over the motives of the cryonics organisations (which are sometimes alleged – with no good evidence – to be motivated by commercial considerations)
- Worries that clients of cryonics organisations will be disproportionately rich, and that these organisations will become obstacles to social change
- Uncertainty over which provider should be preferred.

In principle, strategies are known to deal with each of these factors. As in numerous other fields of life, costs should decline and quality increase as the total number of experiences of a product or service increases. These are known as scale effects.

Hence the desirability of the following goal: *cryonic suspension will be offered to all, on point of death, on the NHS, without requiring individual payments*. Just as no-one needs to pay to be born, no-one should need to pay to be cryonically suspended.

Actions that are likely to increase the number of people signed up for cryonics (and thereby reduce individual costs) include:

- Convincing demonstrations of successful reanimation of larger biological organisms or organs
- Changes in the law concerning euthanasia, to allow people who are approaching death to control the time when cryopreservation can start (this is sometimes known as cryothanasia)
- Storage of cryopreserved bodies at locations throughout the UK, rather than travel needing to be arranged overseas
- Involvement of hospital doctors and other staff in the cryopreservation process, rather than a potentially disruptive handover needing to be made to a team of "standby volunteers".

Another suggestion is that cryopreservation of the brain could be offered by the NHS in return for the other organs in the body being made available for transplantation or scientific research.

Ectogenetic pregnancies on the NHS?

Whereas cryonics (discussed in the previous section) would provide additional choices over the treatment of people at the end of their natural life, ectogenetic pregnancies would provide additional choices for mothers bringing new babies into the world.

The proposed goal is that *pregnancy via ectogenesis will be available to all on the NHS*.

The rationale for the goal is that many women who currently find themselves unable or unwilling to become mothers by natural gestation will be grateful for the opportunity provided by ectogenesis. Coupled with therapies to regenerate ovaries and reverse the menopause, this treatment will provide additional choice to women, beyond existing options such as adoption.

Ectogenetic pregnancies extend and unify two fields of healthcare that already exist:

- IVF: In-Vitro Fertilisation, in which conception takes place outside of the bodies of the parents
- Hospital incubator care of babies that are born prematurely – babies that would otherwise have been too young to survive.

Ectogenetic pregnancies would remove the need for the growing embryo to be implanted inside the mother in between conception and birth. Instead, growth will take place inside a kind of artificial womb.

An indication of the kind of technology that could one day provide artificial wombs is given in the 2017 Nature article "An extra-uterine system to physiologically support the extreme premature lamb"[160]:

> In the developed world, extreme prematurity is the leading cause of neonatal mortality and morbidity due to a combination of organ immaturity and iatrogenic injury. Until now, efforts to extend gestation using extracorporeal systems have achieved limited success. Here we report the development of a system that incorporates a pumpless oxygenator circuit connected to the fetus of a lamb via an umbilical cord interface that is maintained within a closed 'amniotic fluid' circuit that closely reproduces the environment of the womb. We show that fetal lambs that are developmentally equivalent to the extreme premature human infant can be physiologically supported in this extra-uterine device for up to 4 weeks. Lambs on support maintain stable haemodynamics, have normal blood gas and oxygenation parameters and maintain patency of the fetal circulation. With appropriate nutritional support, lambs on the system demonstrate normal somatic growth, lung maturation and brain growth and myelination…
>
> Extreme premature fetal lambs can be consistently supported in an extracorporeal device for up to 4 weeks without apparent physiologic derangement or organ failure.

At the other end of the process, scientists in the United Kingdom have (as reported in the Guardian[161]) have kept embryos alive for 13 days after conception:

> Researchers at Cambridge University… have kept a human embryo alive outside the body for 13 days using a mix of nutrients that mimic conditions in the womb. The embryo survived several days longer than previously observed and research only stopped because they were approaching the 14-day legal limit for the length of time an embryo can be kept in a lab. In other

words, our ethics rather than our technology are now the limiting factor.

The Guardian article continues:

> The key to survival through ectogenesis is reproducing the conditions of the womb. As scientists become better at that, the gap between the longest time embryos can survive and the earliest time a foetus is viable will narrow. When the two timescales meet, we will have the technology for a complete external womb.

However, there are still major obstacles to facilitating total extra-uterine development. It will take some time to fully identify and generate all the biologically active molecules that are incorporated into a developing embryo. It will also be a major challenge to develop a system that facilitates the specialised angiogenesis processes that form a working umbilical cord to connect to the surrogate maternal system, delivering all the elements.

Views vary regarding the desirability of this technology – similar to the heated debates that preceded the availability of IVF in the late 1970s. At that time, it was widely thought that excess psychological pressures would apply to the women, families, and children involved. However, society subsequently developed methods to handle these pressures.

To support this goal, further investment of research would need to be prioritised, in order to provide women with the greater freedoms and opportunities the technology would provide. In parallel, discussion should continue about the social and psychological implications of this technology. An example of a short fictional story that can prompt useful reflection on this topic is the video by Rachel Foley, "Technocratic Birth"[162].

This goal may turn out to be too ambitious for the 2035 time horizon. If further study were to confirm that conclusion, the goal could be revised to the adoption of technology supporting babies that are ever more premature.

Moving forwards

By the way, how can we judge how much change it is credible to imagine can take place in a given time period? That's one of the questions that is included in the FAQ (Frequently Asked Questions) list for RAFT, as contained in the next chapter.

17. FAQ

Please find below answers to questions that have arisen during reviews of RAFT.

Next steps

Q: There's a lot to admire in RAFT 2035. What are the best ways to help this project succeed?

A: The simple summary is: *influence the influencers, educate the educators, and inspire those who can, in turn, inspire others*:

- Organise or take part in RAFT events, both online and offline
- Look for opportunities to have some of the RAFT ideas presented to different audiences, both online and offline
- Explore varying the format and expressions for the ideas, including creative use of graphics, videos, narratives, and memes
- Extend and adapt the ideas for different locales – including translating the material into new languages
- Be ready to offer RAFT ideas in timely response to any news story or publication where the ideas are particularly relevant
- Forge connections with communities where the RAFT ideas can bring new insight.

RAFT is by no means static or complete. It needs to expand and evolve:

- Notice where there are gaps or problems with the RAFT ideas, and consider appropriate responses to these gaps and problems
- Consider developing, not only the 15 original goals, but also similar goals for the ideas in the "bubbling under" category
- Join project teams working on the various interim 2025 targets; highlight clear steps of progress being made, and draw attention to areas where there are hindrances and blockages
- Take part in the preparation and distribution of regular reports for each of the RAFT goals
- Develop political policy recommendations that are aligned with the RAFT vision; ideally, these recommendations will be suitable to slot into the manifestos of various think tanks or political parties, and from there, into legislative programmes around the world
- Plan and carry out specific campaigns based on individual RAFT ideas – campaigns to raise public awareness and alter the public discussion
- Develop processes to welcome and engage people from all walks of life who are keen to assist with RAFT; in this way, help new and old community members alike to find roles whereby they can contribute to individual projects and also grow in accomplishment.

For news about RAFT events and projects, see londonfuturists.com or transpolitica.org.

UK and global versions

Q: Why aren't the goals of RAFT 2035 expressed in global terms? Why the focus on UK-specific metrics?

A: Large projects need to be broken down into manageable chunks. This needs to happen, not only in terms of timescales, but also in terms of locale.

For timescales, the vision of what can be accomplished by 2035 needs to be supported by an understanding of what it is credible to achieve by earlier dates, such as 2025.

Likewise for locale: the vision of an entire world enjoying an abundance of flourishing and transcendence needs to be supported by an understanding of what can be done in each local region:

- An awareness of the current situation
- A set of proposals: practices to be updated, taxes and incentives to be revised, and legislation to be introduced
- An awareness of potential local allies (and local obstacles).

The 2020 version of RAFT – this book – has much to say that is applicable worldwide as well as just in the UK. Subsequent new outputs of the RAFT project are likely to contain additional material addressing specific issues and opportunities around the globe.

Separatism and new cities

Q: Does the metaphor of "raft" suggest that people should organise themselves to live in a separate society, freed from interference from the rest of the world? How does the concept of RAFT connect to ideas such as "seasteading"[163], as featured in (for example) the novel *The Transhumanist Wager*[164] written by Zoltan Istvan?

A: There can be no safety on the earth until all societies feel satisfied and secure. There is no safety in isolationism. Risks from climate change, environmental destruction, and military conflict cannot be avoided by retreating to a supposedly secure vantage point at some remote location on the earth. Instead, the metaphor of RAFT emphasises the idea of a journey:

- From the present, deeply unstable situation, in which there is lots of dangerous turbulence
- To a future, in which the turbulence has been tamed, and in which an abundance of flourishing is available *to everyone*
- With a fast speed for the journey being possible by taking wise advantage of the fast-flowing turbulence.

However, there *is* a role to be played by new communities which embody a selection of the changes that RAFT foresees as deeply desirable. These communities can serve as examples that will change the mind of the wider public about what is possible and what is desirable. These communities can also carry out important experiments that are not possible within traditional society.

Capitalism and fiat money

Q: Why is there no goal in RAFT to displace capitalism or to abolish fiat money? Surely a world of abundance is one in which there is no role for money?

A: RAFT warns against each of two fundamentalist extremes: the extreme that says capitalism (and the free market) is the best possible kind of social system, and the extreme that says capitalism (and the free market) is deeply corrosive, and must be dismantled.

Instead, RAFT endorses what is called the "mixed economy". The operation of the economy and the financial system should be treated as a means, not an end in itself. These systems should be monitored and, in key aspects, steered and controlled by society as a whole.

There is nothing intrinsically wrong with use of the pricing mechanism, nor in the creation of fiat money (along with interest-bearing debt). What is wrong is when society gives too much focus on economic and financial metrics.

Hence the vital interim goals in RAFT for the development of a replacement of GDP, to serve as a better guide on how the economy and the financial system should be evaluated.

As for a potential ongoing role for money: even if all the items needed for a high quality of life are abundant, there will invariably be some novel goods or services that are still in a situation of comparative scarcity. It is for these goods and services where an evolved version of our current monetary system can still play a useful role.

Positivity and realism

Q: Why does RAFT highlight the risks of potential civilisational catastrophe, rather than focusing on the many very positive trends in human flourishing? Rather than emphasising what looks like an emergency survival narrative – a narrative that carries destructive psychological tendencies – wouldn't it be better to highlight ongoing innovations in products and services, that are improving human wellbeing?

A: As the opening pages of RAFT point out,

> Whilst some social metrics indicate major progress, others indicate major setbacks. The claim "You've never had it so good" coexists with the counterclaim "It's going to be worse than ever". To add to the bewilderment, there seems to be lots of evidence confirming both views.
>
> The metrics that should cause major concern include:
>
> - A surge in extreme weather events
> - A potential step change in the pace of species extinction
> - A decline in many countries in average healthspan
> - A serious rise in mental illnesses
> - Easier access to a variety of "weapons of mass destruction"
> - A decline in the proportion of citizens seeing democracy as desirable
> - An increase in the willingness of electors to tolerate and even celebrate rampant untruthfulness by politicians
> - A rise in the share of wealth and power controlled by the richest fraction of a percent of the population
> - Greater ability by organisations to manipulate the thinking of members of the public, reducing autonomy
> - A growth in enthusiasm for outlandish conspiracy theories and pseudoscience.

What needs to be considered isn't just a linear extrapolation of these trends, but potential *exponential magnifications resulting from feedback loops*. There's also the question of the convergence and collisions of several of these trends. Finally, there's the global, hyperspeed always-on multi-connected nature of today's society: advance warning can actually accelerate the trends. It's not just variant new biological viruses that should worry us; variant new mental viruses can cause global chaos too.

We need to hold in our minds, simultaneously, the enormous potential of new technology, as well as the enormous risks it poses. Two recipes for failure in any social change programme are:

- Too much doom and gloom: driving people into despair
- Too much naive optimism: failing to prepare sufficient solutions to existential dangers.

History shows many examples of societies collapsing, from heights that previously seemed impregnable[165]. These previous collapses were local, but a collapse in the near future would likely be global in scale. It might provide a short-term psychological boost to deny this possibility, but such a denial would be deeply irresponsible. At the same time, it's important to be able to move on quickly from appraising the seriousness of various risks, to exploring credible solutions to these risks.

In other words: it's true that human ingenuity can accomplish wonders. However, it's important that our human ingenuity is applied to what are the most pressing problems. Lack of attention to these problems may mean we make significant progress on matters of lesser importance, en route to being overwhelmed by a disaster that makes all that progress irrelevant.

Interest from politicians

Q: Aren't politicians mainly preoccupied by shorter term matters and comparatively small-minded visions, instead of the potential for the larger changes in human flourishing covered in RAFT? What's going to persuade politicians to pay any attention to the RAFT initiatives, and to reallocate public resources accordingly?

A: Politicians vary considerably. Within each party, alongside some politicians whose horizons have shrunk, there are other politicians who are open in principle to new ideas for radical improvements in the human condition. All that's needed is to find the right communications pathway.

There are two ways in which such politicians can be persuaded to give serious consideration to ideas such as are contained in RAFT:

- Politicians are sensitive to public opinion. When there is evidence of a change in the public mood, politicians are ready to start exploring views aligned with this change. Therefore, when members of the general public talk and write more often about the goals contained in RAFT, we can expect growing interest in these goals from politicians as well.
- At least some politicians are sensitive, not only to *the current public opinion*, but to *what they believe could shortly become public opinion*. If the advisers to these politicians forward reports about what is being

said by emerging future thought leaders (including present-day students, or even school students), it raises the possibility of those politicians acting not just as *followers* of these emerging new opinions, but as perceived *shapers* and *leaders* of these opinions.

Accordingly, to change the minds of politicians, supporters of RAFT 2035 should seek to find ways to raise awareness of the merits of the RAFT goals among various other thought leaders in society. This can be summarised (as stated earlier) as "influence the influencers, educate the educators, and inspire those who can, in turn, inspire others". In time, various politicians will, likewise, be influenced, educated, and inspired. Once this happens, we will start to see growing support for policy proposals that will accelerate the steps in the RAFT roadmap.

Institutionalised resistance

Q: Even if individual political leaders are supportive in principle of the RAFT ideas, won't any radical reform initiatives be undermined by forces within the political and legal systems which are determined to resist any significant changes? How will the huge forces of institutionalised resistance be overcome?

A: Previous positive examples that can act as inspiration include the abolition of slavery, the granting of votes to women, the establishment of the welfare state, and the legalisation of same-sex marriage.

Moreover, "the establishment" is far from being a uniform entity. Individual media proprietors can be persuaded to break from the pack, and to give more voice to alternate points of view. Some parts of the legal and political system may indeed be inclined to resist radical change, but other parts can swing behind it – especially when they become convinced of the deep merits of the new proposals.

Key to building a powerful coalition that has the strength to overcome institutionalised resistance will be to highlight the ways in which the RAFT vision will benefit *everyone* – even including those "winners" in the current system whose hands are currently on (or near) the levers of power:

- Those present-day "winners" may end up, in the RAFT vision, having less of a *relative* advantage over the rest of society; they will no longer have control over resources that are (say) thousands of times the scale of the resources available to the ordinary person.
- However, those present-day "winners" will end up better *in absolute terms* than at present – especially when taking into account the steep drop in the societal hostility that is induced by present-day inequalities of opportunity. With abundance for all, there will no longer be the constant fear of an uprising that seeks vengeance.

A new political party

Q: Should support be given to a new political party which focuses on the RAFT goals? How about the UK's Transhumanist Party, where the RAFT ideas first took shape?

A: In countries with single-MP first-past-the-post voting systems, such as the UK, any new political party faces tremendous difficulties in attracting enough votes to place an MP into parliament. Foreseeing the unlikelihood of a candidate becoming an MP, voters will feel strong pressures to avoid casting their vote for such a candidate, seeing it as a wasted vote.

Until the voting system is overhauled (as proposed as part of Goal 14), new parties will, accordingly, face an enormous uphill battle.

That's one reason to avoid putting energy into a new, separate political party. It's a reason, instead, to seek to influence people in all existing parties to adopt at least some of the RAFT goals.

On the other hand, candidates standing for a new party – even if they have no realistic prospects of being elected – can gain useful publicity, and raise more awareness for the causes they champion.

Mind, spirit, and transcendence

Q: Why does RAFT talk about rejuvenating not only the brain and the mind, but also the spirit? Isn't "spirit" an unhelpful, unscientific term? On similar lines, in what sense is the word "transcendence" being used?

A: The word "spirit" is used as a shorthand for saying that there's more to human inner life than our conscious thinking. The rejuvenation of spirit that RAFT envisions is the elevation in human character and disposition covered by Goal 2, and includes deeper levels of calmness, compassion, connectedness, and creativity.

Indeed, Goal 2 has a claim to being the most fundamental of the entire set of 15 goals.

The vision is that *all of us* will become able to routinely reach (and surpass) the heights of consciousness demonstrated by aspects of the lives of great composers, dancers, poets, artists, craftsmakers, surgeons, mathematicians, adepts, saints, meditators, mystics, and peacemakers – without falling foul of the obsessive character traits that sometimes accompany these personalities.

The vision is "transcendence" in the sense that humanity can soar beyond the limits which have hitherto restricted our experience and ability. We inherited these limits from blind evolution, from out-dated cultural norms, and from pre-scientific systems of philosophy. But the next fifteen years can see an acceleration of the creative redesign of ourselves as individuals, as social beings, and as cosmic voyagers.

Towards 2025

Q: What is a headline summary of the various interim targets which RAFT outlines for 2025?

A: The interim targets fall into three broad categories:

1. Demonstrations of tangible progress with new technologies or new solutions – progress that should increasingly change people's minds about the speed at which yet more progress might be possible
2. Clarifications of potential new systems, metrics, or processes, via which greater flourishing can be made available to all, in ways that protect and elevate human values
3. Miscellaneous additional milestones en route to human transcendence.

In the category "demonstrations of tangible progress with new technologies or new solutions":

- Demonstrate mid-age rejuvenation of animals with much smaller lifespans than humans (Goal 1)
- Demonstrate long-lasting effectiveness of some of the proposed new "transformational technology" solutions for improved mental wellbeing (Goal 2)
- Demonstrate the effectiveness of at least some elements of edtech, in reducing costs whilst delivering higher quality education (Goal 5)
- Demonstrate "full taste parity" of selected alternatives to slaughtered meat (Goal 11)
- Demonstrate tangible progress in at least one of the smaller fusion projects (Goal 13)

In the category "clarifications of potential new systems, metrics, or processes, via which greater flourishing can be made available to all":

- Establish a society-wide understanding of the principles of the longevity dividend, and of the measures that can be taken to quickly reduce the costs of rejuvenation therapies so that everyone can benefit from them (Goal 1)
- Update the legislation which unnecessarily constrains the wise use of some of "transformational technology" solutions – especially legislation covering psychedelic drugs and other psychoactive substances (Goal 2)
- Agree an initial series of "cost of living well" indices (Goal 3)
- Agree the basic elements of a revised social contract in which paid employment loses the

prime position it has in present-day society (Goal 3)

- Agree a replacement for the GDP index as the guiding light for evaluating the success of the economy: rather than focusing on increasing the financial value of goods produced and consumed, we need an alternative which better measures the basis for all-round human flourishing (Goal 4) and which fully incorporates factors known as "externalities", that is the impacts of economic activities which are presently excluded from valuation (Goals 9 and 10)
- Agree the core of a transformed educational syllabus focused on new life opportunities – an education fit for the 2020s and beyond (Goal 5)
- Agree basic principles of the design and operation of systems for "trustable monitoring" (Goal 6)
- Agree basic principles of the design and operation of systems for "international trustable monitoring" which should, among other points, highlight measures to constrain any runaway escalation of adoption of lethal autonomous weapons (Goal 7)
- Establish a commitment from a majority of the countries in the United Nations to an updated version of the Universal Declaration of Human Rights which takes fully into account the remarkable transformational nature of the technologies highlighted in RAFT (Goal 7)
- Reach a general understanding of the economic case for open borders, and the types of constraints

that need to be applied so that the benefits significantly outweigh the drawbacks (Goal 8)

- Agree a statement of the "core values of all UK residents", highlighting those features of law and practice which are regarded as key to harmony and flourishing within the UK, and also making it clear which elements of human and transhuman variation and diversity should be accepted or even encouraged – and which elements of diversity should be resisted (Goal 8)
- Obtain majority public support for the design of a system to replace first past the post election (Goal 14)
- Agree an understanding of the actual purpose of politicians, including the key role of the public sector in a mixed economy, and also including awareness of the role of industrial strategy (Goal 14)
- Reach an agreement on limits on the roles that can be played by commercially owned AI, that recognises the potential large contribution that could be made by commercially owned software, without being naive about the risks (Goal 15)
- Reach an agreement on the principles of "ethical AI": what are the features which an AI *could* be built to include, but which will *need to be excluded or curtailed*, for the sake of true human flourishing? (Goal 15)

And in the category "miscellaneous additional milestones en route to human transcendence":

- Establish a reliable, respected source of information about the true health benefits and risks of different types of diet and different kinds of accommodation (Goal 4) and about the true environmental benefits and risks of different types of human actions (Goals 9 and 10)
- Advance practical initiatives to understand and reduce particular types of crime, starting with the types of crime (such as violent crime) that have the biggest negative impact on people's lives (Goal 6)
- Clarify the range of health benefits from alternatives to slaughtered meat, bearing in mind that consumption of meat has been linked to many diseases (Goal 11)
- Humans will walk on the Moon again, helping humanity to rediscover a sense of cosmic delight, with these new visitors to our nearest cosmic neighbour including women as well as men, and people from multiple different nationalities (Goal 12)
- A round trip mission to Mars will be underway, using robots, to collect rock samples and then return them to Earth (Goal 12)
- Complete the construction of ITER facilities, as per its current committed schedule, without any further delays (Goal 13).

As each year passes, up to the end of 2025, annual progress reports should be produced for each of these interim targets, highlighting:

- Measures of success and failure over the preceding 12 months
- Any new opportunities and risks arising
- Any reasons for changes in the targets, or for the adoption of new milestones (with intended completion date either before or after 2025).

Depending on your own special interests and expertise, please consider assisting with one or more of these projects.

An honest assessment of progress

Q: How can we judge how much change it is credible to imagine can take place in a given time period? How can we avoid being misled by our own biases and wishes? How can we look honestly and soberly at actual progress and setbacks, free from rose-tinted glasses or overly cynical expectations? In a world of increasing "fake news", where can we find a secure bedrock of reliable data?

A: The effort to transcend bias and wishful thinking is one of the most important for the wellbeing of humanity. As mentioned during the discussion of Goal 15, two sets of tools can help: the tools of collective intelligence, and the tools of artificial intelligence.

In both cases, it will increase the chance of a good outcome from using these tools if a diverse group of individuals can pool their insights and findings in a knowledge-base of data and analysis. One example of such a knowledge-base is Wikipedia, though there are questions about the criteria it imposes for what counts as worthy of inclusion. Another example is H+Pedia[166], whose mission statement includes the following:

> H+Pedia aims to follow the principles of Wikipedia. At the same time, the H+Pedia editorial team seek to demonstrate greater awareness and appreciation of transhumanism and radical futurism. This will be reflected by the inclusion in H+Pedia of material which might not pass the Wikipedia tests for notability, as currently applied by Wikipedia editors.

The further development of H+Pedia, or systems with a similar intent, is likely to feature prominently in future RAFT progress reports.

18. Acknowledgements

RAFT 2035 has been greatly improved due to comments, questions, and suggestions raised by a number of friends, colleagues, and people who share an interest in at least some of the same ideas.

Many thanks are due to: Anders Sandberg, Tony Czarnecki, Dan Elton, Jenina Bas, Mathieu Gosselin, Julian Snape, Alexander Karran, Yfke Laanstra, Thomas O'Carroll, Mark Waser, José Cordeiro, Dean Bubley, Calum Chace, Catarina Lamm, Johannon Ben Zion, Marc Roux, Andrew Vladimirov, Kim Solez, Simon Stiel, Peter Rothman, Corinne Coles, and Michael Arnell.

All errors and infelicities that remain are due to the lead author, David W. Wood.

Communities matter

In addition to thanking individuals, it's appropriate to highlight a number of communities whose members and events have assisted in multiple ways in stimulating or advancing the thinking contained in RAFT 2035.

In each case, these communities are worth further attention. They all have activities relevant to multiple different RAFT 2035 goals:

- Humanity+[167]: "An international nonprofit membership organisation that advocates the ethical use of technology, such as artificial intelligence, to expand human capacities. In other words, we want people to be better than well. This is the goal of transhumanism."

- The IEET (Institute for Ethics and Emerging Technologies)[168]: "Formed to study and debate vital questions such as: Which technologies, especially new ones, are likely to have the greatest impact on human beings and human societies in the 21st century? And what ethical issues do those technologies and their applications raise for humans, our civilisation, and our world?"
- The Millennium Project[169]: "A global foresight network of nodes, information, and software, functioning as a think tank on behalf of humanity, not on behalf of a government, an issue, or an ideology. Created to improve humanity's prospects for building a better future"
- The World Future Society[170]: "Our mission is to awaken the Futurist Mindset in everyone. Whether you're focused on social impact, creating a disruptive business, or exploring exponential technology, we believe there is a futurist in each of us."
- The Alternative UK[171]: "Beneath the democratic deficit lies an imagination deficit. Our purpose is to catalyse a new politics that goes far beyond our current reality. We focus on engagement more than elections, on values over ideology, on futures that include, not exclude. We care about solutions, challenges – and great questions."
- Nesta[172]: "An innovation foundation. For us, innovation means turning bold ideas into reality. It also means changing lives for the better. We work in areas where there are big challenges facing society, from the frontiers of personalised healthcare to

stretched public services and a fast-changing jobs market."

- The RSA (Royal Society for the encouragement of Arts, Manufactures and Commerce)[173]: "Through our ideas, research and a 30,000 strong Fellowship we are a global community of proactive problem solvers, sharing powerful ideas, carrying out cutting-edge research and building networks and opportunities for people to collaborate, influence and demonstrate practical solutions to realise change."
- The US Transhumanist Party[174]: "Putting science, health, and technology at the forefront of politics. We seek to achieve the next, greatest era of our civilisation, which will require constructive solutions to the problems of our current era. All of these problems can be solved if we look away from the political trench warfare of today and up toward a far brighter future."
- London Futurists[175]: "The next few years are likely to bring unprecedented change. Our mission is 'Serious analysis of radical scenarios for the next 3-40 years.' Our meetings and projects explore both the potential upsides, and the potential downsides, of these scenarios."

For communities that are focused on smaller numbers of areas, see the "For Further Information" sections at the end of each of the main chapters in this book.

Design matters

The cover design of this book incorporates photography by Pixabay member Couleur[176], used with gratitude!

About the footnotes

Note: a clickable version of the following set of references can be found online at https://transpolitica.org/projects/raft-2035/footnotes/.

---

1 https://www.ons.gov.uk/peoplepopulationandcommunity/healthandsocialcare/healthandlifeexpectancies/bulletins/healthstatelifeexpectanciesuk/2016to2018

2 https://www.finder.com/life-insurance/odds-of-dying

3 https://www.lifespan.io/road-maps/the-rejuvenation-roadmap/

4 https://juvenescence.ltd/

5 https://www.ft.com/content/30bb0752-6d5e-11e8-92d3-6c13e5c92914

6 https://parteifuergesundheitsforschung.de/about_us

7 https://scholar.harvard.edu/cutler/publications/substantial-health-and-economic-returns-delayed-aging-may-warrant-new-focus

8 https://www.undoing-aging.org/

9 https://www.lifespan.io/

10 https://www.sens.org/

11 https://parteifuergesundheitsforschung.de/about_us

12 https://www.longevityinternational.org/

13 https://lifespanbook.com/

14 https://www.goodreads.com/book/show/45358658-nano-comes-to-life

15 https://www.goodreads.com/book/show/46404234-the-switch

16 https://academic.oup.com/ppar/article/29/4/116/5585525

17 https://www.goodreads.com/book/show/34397791-the-longevity-code

18 https://www.goodreads.com/book/show/36112397-juvenescence

[19] https://theabolitionofaging.com/
[20] https://www.goodreads.com/book/show/26835475-the-aging-gap-between-species
[21] https://www.leafscience.org/ending-aging/
[22] https://humanhealthspan.com/
[23] http://digital.nhs.uk/catalogue/PUB21748
[24] https://www.mind.org.uk/information-support/types-of-mental-health-problems/statistics-and-facts-about-mental-health/how-common-are-mental-health-problems/
[25] https://www.mentalhealth.org.uk/statistics/mental-health-statistics-suicide
[26] https://www.ncbi.nlm.nih.gov/pmc/articles/PMC3131101/
[27] https://www.goodreads.com/book/show/478.Bowling_Alone
[28] https://www.goodreads.com/book/show/33584231-the-strange-death-of-europe
[29] https://www.newyorker.com/magazine/2017/05/29/james-mattis-a-warrior-in-washington
[30] https://transtechlab.org/
[31] https://siyli.org/
[32] https://www.imperial.ac.uk/news/190994/imperial-launches-worlds-first-centre-psychedelics/
[33] https://maps.org/
[34] http://www.cohack.org/
[35] https://www.collectivepsychology.org/
[36] https://www.happierlivesinstitute.org/
[37] https://www.goodreads.com/book/show/18878780-the-righteous-mind
[38] https://www.goodreads.com/book/show/33844386-the-myth-gap
[39] https://www.goodreads.com/book/show/30317415-stealing-fire

[40] https://www.goodreads.com/book/show/34466963-why-we-sleep

[41] https://www.goodreads.com/book/show/36613747-how-to-change-your-mind

[42] https://transpolitica.org/projects/transcending-politics/work-and-purpose/

[43] https://transpolitica.org/projects/transcending-politics/

[44] https://www.goodreads.com/book/show/20578356-with-liberty-and-dividends-for-all

[45] https://www.goodreads.com/book/show/22928874-rise-of-the-robots

[46] https://www.goodreads.com/book/show/31176295-the-economic-singularity

[47] https://www.goodreads.com/book/show/34466958-bullshit-jobs

[48] https://www.goodreads.com/book/show/40717359-hedge

[49] https://www.goodreads.com/book/show/36204293-the-war-on-normal-people

[50] https://www.goodreads.com/book/show/50092989-automation-and-utopia

[51] http://www.millennium-project.org/projects/workshops-on-future-of-worktechnology-2050-scenarios/

[52] https://www.ohchr.org/en/NewsEvents/Pages/DisplayNews.aspx?NewsID=23881

[53] https://www.bbc.co.uk/news/uk-46662909

[54] https://en.wikipedia.org/wiki/List_of_countries_by_homeless_population

[55] https://www.theguardian.com/world/2015/apr/30/chinese-construction-firm-erects-57-storey-skyscraper-in-19-days

[56] https://www.ons.gov.uk/peoplepopulationandcommunity/wellbeing/
[57] https://transpolitica.org/projects/abundance-manifesto/6-an-abundance-of-food-and-water/
[58] https://transpolitica.org/projects/abundance-manifesto/
[59] https://www.economist.com/leaders/2020/01/16/home-ownership-is-the-wests-biggest-economic-policy-mistake
[60] https://builtincommon.org/
[61] https://www.goodreads.com/book/show/34959327-the-wizard-and-the-prophet
[62] https://www.goodreads.com/book/show/31258173-food-fight
[63] https://www.goodreads.com/book/show/15843186-radical-abundance
[64] https://www.goodreads.com/book/show/13187824-abundance
[65] https://www.khanacademy.org/
[66] https://www.duolingo.com/
[67] https://www.42.us.org/
[68] https://www.theschooloflife.com/
[69] https://www.goodreads.com/book/show/38820046-21-lessons-for-the-21st-century
[70] https://edtechdigest.com/
[71] https://www.goodreads.com/book/show/2546421.Disrupting_Class
[72] https://www.youtube.com/watch?v=dqTTojTija8
[73] https://www.youtube.com/watch?v=zDZFcDGpL4U
[74] https://www.ons.gov.uk/peoplepopulationandcommunity/crimeandjustice/bulletins/crimeinenglandandwales/yearendingdecember2018

---

75 https://www.goodreads.com/book/show/38212153-click-here-to-kill-everybody

76 https://www.goodreads.com/book/show/22318398-future-crimes

77 https://www.goodreads.com/book/show/96477.The_Transparent_Society

78 https://pjammer.livejournal.com/151502.html

79 https://www.goodreads.com/book/show/40180025-army-of-none

80 https://spectrum.ieee.org/automaton/robotics/artificial-intelligence/why-you-should-fear-slaughterbots-a-response

81 https://www.goodreads.com/book/show/16700084-divided-nations

82 https://www.gov.uk/government/organisations/migration-advisory-committee

83 https://www.independent.co.uk/news/business/analysis-and-features/immigration-migration-advisory-committee-productivity-skill-gdp-brexit-a8542841.html

84 https://www.economist.com/the-world-if/2017/07/13/a-world-of-free-movement-would-be-78-trillion-richer

85 https://en.wikipedia.org/wiki/Open_border#List_of_groups_of_states_with_common_open_borders

86 https://en.wikipedia.org/wiki/Leviathan_(Hobbes_book)

87 https://www.goodreads.com/book/show/33584231-the-strange-death-of-europe

88 https://www.goodreads.com/book/show/40876575-utopia-for-realists

89 https://www.goodreads.com/book/show/43999257-what-do-we-know-and-what-should-we-do-about-immigration
90 https://www.goodreads.com/book/show/8856773-exceptional-people
91 https://transpolitica.org/projects/abundance-manifesto/4-determining-priorities/
92 https://transpolitica.org/projects/abundance-manifesto/
93 https://www.amazon.co.uk/Democracy-Human-Federation-Coexisting-Superintelligence/dp/1689622334/
94 https://www.gov.uk/government/statistics/uks-carbon-footprint
95 https://www.atlanticcouncil.org/blogs/new-atlanticist/climate-change-as-a-threat-multiplier/
96 https://www.theguardian.com/environment/2018/may/23/hitting-toughest-climate-target-will-save-world-30tn-in-damages-analysis-shows
97 https://transpolitica.org/projects/abundance-manifesto/5-an-abundance-of-energy/
98 https://transpolitica.org/projects/abundance-manifesto/
99 https://www.edx.org/course/making-sense-of-climate-science-denial
100 https://www.goodreads.com/book/show/41552709-the-uninhabitable-earth
101 https://www.goodreads.com/book/show/45897523-blowout
102 https://www.goodreads.com/book/show/40538538-goliath
103 https://www.goodreads.com/book/show/36722606-taming-the-sun
104 https://www.goodreads.com/book/show/32075449-the-ends-of-the-world

---

105 https://www.goodreads.com/book/show/16291969-the-infinite-resource
106 https://www.goodreads.com/book/show/21913812-this-changes-everything
107 https://www.goodreads.com/book/show/7799004-merchants-of-doubt
108 https://www.goodreads.com/book/show/43822733-more-from-less
109 https://www.goodreads.com/book/show/29214420-doughnut-economics
110 https://www.stockholmresilience.org/research/planetary-boundaries/planetary-boundaries/about-the-research/the-nine-planetary-boundaries.html
111 https://www.theguardian.com/commentisfree/2019/jun/05/eating-meat-future-socially-unacceptable-obsolete
112 https://www.adamsmith.org/research/dont-have-a-cow-man-the-prospects-for-lab-grown-meat
113 https://www.goodreads.com/book/show/17160008-feral
114 https://www.goodreads.com/book/show/36101304-clean-meat
115 https://www.hedweb.com/gene-drives/index.html
116 https://www.meatable.com/
117 https://www.peta.org.uk/living/vegan-meats/
118 https://archive.nytimes.com/www.nytimes.com/library/national/science/nasa/122568sci-nasa-macleish.html
119 https://www.saga.co.uk/magazine/entertainment/nostalgia/moon-landing-anniversary
120 https://www.bbc.co.uk/news/science-environment-48912458

121 https://www.ida.org/-/media/feature/publications/e/ev/evaluation-of-a-human-mission-to-mars-by-2033/d-10510.ashx
122 http://100photos.time.com/photos/nasa-earthrise-apollo-8
123 https://www.pbs.org/wgbh/americanexperience/features/moon-earth-moon/
124 https://www.marssociety.org/
125 https://www.imdb.com/title/tt6223974/
126 https://www.goodreads.com/book/show/42046662-the-case-for-space
127 https://www.iter.org/
128 http://www.psfc.mit.edu/sparc
129 https://www.tokamakenergy.co.uk/
130 https://firstlightfusion.com/
131 https://www.ft.com/content/a8d0a7e4-20e3-11ea-b8a1-584213ee7b2b
132 https://www.ipsos.com/ipsos-mori/en-uk/trust-politicians-falls-sending-them-spiralling-back-bottom-ipsos-mori-veracity-index
133 https://www.edelman.com/trust-barometer
134 https://www.europeansocialsurvey.org/data/themes.html?t=politics
135 https://en.wikipedia.org/wiki/First-past-the-post_voting#List_of_former_FPTP_countries
136 https://transpolitica.org/projects/transcending-politics/democracy-and-inclusion/
137 https://transpolitica.org/projects/transcending-politics/
138 https://www.electoral-reform.org.uk/
139 https://www.goodreads.com/book/show/12158480-why-nations-fail
140 https://www.goodreads.com/book/show/25814409-american-amnesia

---

141 https://www.goodreads.com/book/show/39979237-moneyland
142 https://transpolitica.org/2019/12/10/a-reliability-index-for-politicians/
143 https://en.wikipedia.org/wiki/John_Dalberg-Acton,_1st_Baron_Acton
144 https://blogs.scientificamerican.com/guest-blog/how-the-science-of-blue-lies-may-explain-trumps-support/
145 https://www.goodreads.com/book/show/46758636-don-t-be-evil
146 https://www.goodreads.com/book/show/44767248-human-compatible
147 https://www.goodreads.com/book/show/40909439-zucked
148 https://www.goodreads.com/book/show/44154569-the-ai-does-not-hate-you
149 https://www.goodreads.com/book/show/39383637-the-blockchain-and-the-new-architecture-of-trust
150 https://www.goodreads.com/book/show/26195941-the-age-of-surveillance-capitalism
151 https://www.goodreads.com/book/show/39403470-the-people-vs-tech
152 https://www.goodreads.com/book/show/38819346-future-politics
153 https://www.goodreads.com/book/show/36204268-superminds
154 https://en.wikipedia.org/wiki/Bubbling_Under_Hot_100
155 https://www.cryonics.org/resources/scientists-open-letter-on-cryonics
156 https://www.ncbi.nlm.nih.gov/pmc/articles/PMC4620520/
157 https://www.cryonics.org/ci-landing/
158 https://alcor.org/BecomeMember/scheduleA.html
159 https://www.alcor.org/cases.html

---

[160] https://www.nature.com/articles/ncomms15112

[161] https://www.theguardian.com/lifeandstyle/2017/sep/04/artifical-womb-women-ectogenesis-baby-fertility

[162] https://vimeo.com/329327598

[163] https://www.seasteading.org/about/

[164] https://www.goodreads.com/book/show/17728761-the-transhumanist-wager

[165] https://www.goodreads.com/book/show/477.Collapse_of_Complex_Societies

[166] https://hpluspedia.org/

[167] https://humanityplus.org/

[168] https://ieet.org/

[169] https://themp.org/

[170] https://www.worldfuture.org/

[171] https://www.thealternative.org.uk/

[172] https://www.nesta.org.uk/

[173] https://www.thersa.org/

[174] https://transhumanist-party.org/

[175] https://londonfuturists.com/

[176] https://pixabay.com/photos/wave-sea-water-blue-surf-1215449/

Printed in Poland
by Amazon Fulfillment
Poland Sp. z o.o., Wrocław

53751544R00115